Bent, Not Broken

Lynn Schriner

ISBN: 0-75961-108-4

This book is printed on acid free paper.

1stBooks – rev. 3/30/01

Dance as though
No one is watching you

Love as though you
Have never been hurt before

Sing as though no one
Can hear you

Live as though heaven
Is on earth

Author Unknown

Acknowledgments.

To all those who have at times carried me, though they themselves were tired

To Jesus, the Author and Finisher of my life

To my father, who is my hero

To my mother, who is my teacher

To Victoria, who is the editor of not only this book, but also my life

To my dearest Joey, who is my greatest fan, and whose love amazes me

And to my family and friends, who have been so much a part of me

Thank you.

God rewards the faithful.

Dedication

To those who suffer
To the hungry
To the sick
To the lonely
To the hopeless
To the orphans

I wrote this book for you

*Fifty percent of my share of this book will go to the precious
orphans in Haiti.*

To learn to see, to learn to hear, you must do this: go into the wilderness alone.

Don Jose Matsuwa

PROLOGUE

The city is full of the energy of a million people who are forced to live on top of, next to and below one another, sharing things as intimate as air, as moving as music, or shouting or crying. You share time and space with total strangers, in a movement so swift through the rush of traffic or the push in a crowd. A stranger sits beside you and smokes; a neighbor, nameless and unknown, calls chemical trucks to spray the lawn, the bugs, the weeds; while another a few blocks away begins to gasp for air and knows not why.

In the heart of downtown, as you exit a café, a musician sits solitary with his instrument, playing with his hat set on a street covered in layers of humanity. He seeks to perform for his next bottle of comfort and escape, and you drop change from your cappuccino into his hat, hoping he will buy a meal instead.

You rush to the nearest mall, the size of a college campus, searching for the greatest gift ever. You find yourself on an obstacle course, moving this way and that, occasionally bumping shoulders and swaying to miss this baby carriage or that weary shopper, looking into windows and wishing.

Your eyes grow wary as you see a group of youths, faded into themselves, absorbed, oblivious, unattended. Some have scarred their faces and bodies, pierced and cut and tattooed, with hair taking on unnatural shades of pink and green. They view you with distaste, and if empowered by numbers even intimidate with gestures or words…and suddenly the mall becomes small. I remember the days of my own youth, and find that somehow the young of today have crossed into a place of apathy and danger, a place that I cannot understand, and therefore I find within my heart fear.

The city with its million people would be a fine place if I was healthy and strong, but in the winter of my forty second year, in a weak and vulnerable place, my husband Joey and I headed south, to find another way to live.

I have decided to stick with love; hate is too great a burden to bear.

Martin Luther King, Jr.

ONE

I waited forty-one years to find my husband. Joey, with his laid back manner and infinite patience, his green eyes and sweet ways, was a perfect compliment to me. I had to grow into him, like a child with a new pair of shoes. They were the shoes I had always wanted, but I found I couldn't wear them comfortably at first. I had to wear two pairs of socks and still I got blisters. Eventually those shoes walked me down smooth roads and rocky cliffs, waded with me through deep and rushing currents, and cushioned me across the hot highways of my life. But there was a definite breaking in period.

Our first year of marriage took us beyond anything we could have imagined. We had a record courtship (eight days), before being thrust into a year that tested us as if we were going for a PhD in marriage without ever having completed high school.

Joey had been married before. She had left him high and dry in a motel on the east coast. Though pregnant with his baby, she refused reconciliation, and lost the child. After we were married, and she found herself in another relationship that was not working for her, she wrote and called Joe, wanting to get back together. We stood together and wrote her a letter, asking her to move on and find her own blessing. Joe had become involved in a lawsuit, which resulted in bankruptcy. His mother and father found great fault with me, and let it be known. We felt adrift and uncertain in our first few months of hell within our "till death do us part" commitment. Marriage was a test of strength: seeing Joe without his teeth which had to be pulled shortly after we said "I do" because of an accident in a tank during maneuvers in the military, seeing me swollen like a chipmunk after having a tooth pulled, the reality of PMS and jobs that pay twenty thousand less than your last job. We had no honeymoon, no time to court or find romance before reality slammed us down. It was a painful time, a growing time, a time of soul searching and compromise. We found that there were never two people so different. Within those differences we had to find compromise, safety, truth and heart. He was sweeter at first, trying to make everything work out between us. He was the peacemaker. I was caught in an illness that had left me coldcocked and fragile. The more fragile I got, the tougher I got about the little things.

After close to five years of marriage, we are beginning to understand why God had us marry so quickly. Marriage for us has been a long lesson and a long healing time. Two wounded people coming together and trying to live in peace through fires that burn has all the makings of a soap opera. Most characters run when the fires burn or the waters come crashing in. Had we been dating, we would have. But our marriage vows are something we believe in and take very seriously. So we said our vows under the watchful eye of our God in heaven, who we believe (to this day) put us together.

We stand today solid as ground can be after four seasons of testing. Joey (as tangled as his life was when we came together) has a bevy of female fans, because he is truly the best husband a girl could ever wish for. I have never felt so securely loved.

We are driving one day in the old GMC pickup. I'm telling him some story, used to having to defend myself and my position. I begin to do that, and he cuts me off short (a thing he never does).

"Don't defend yourself to me," he says, watching the road and wiping his brow. "You never have to, you should know that by now."

I realize that my instinct is to defend, and with a sigh and a smile I lean back against the seat. "Really?" I ask, smiling. "You're always on my side?"

He turns his head just then and the light catches his eyes. "Always," he says.

I remember the day we eloped, one brilliant Sunday in June. We had looked in the yellow pages and found a name listed under "Clergy."

"The reverend is booked for weddings through the summer," his wife had stated in a sweet voice over the phone.

"Oh, ok, well then thank..." I tried to finish but she interrupted me.

"Give me your phone number and I'll ask him. Just maybe, you never know...but dear, I wouldn't count on it."

"Ok ma'am, thanks," I said, eyeing Joey. I put the receiver down in the cradle feeling a little relieved.

"Well, perhaps we really shouldn't get married so soon." It was what we both thought, but what we both felt was entirely different. That morning in church, listening to a sermon on destiny, we both felt we were to be married, and soon.

"I guess I didn't really hear from God like I thought." Joey was passing me the salt when the phone rang.

"The Reverend will marry you at five o'clock," the sweet voice said. I looked at the clock; it was three.

"Joey!" I whooped and hollered. "He can marry us at five!"

Joey's green eyes looked into mine. "Well let's get a move on." He smiled.

We made a mad dash to showers. I had just bought Joey a blue jean shirt, so he wore that. I wore a blue jean dress; we both wore beaded Indian chokers he had made. On the way we stopped and bought a bouquet of dried flowers. As we raced our way up the mountainside's windy roads, we held hands and prayed. When we arrived, at exactly five o'clock, we found that the Reverend owned a huge game preserve.

We walked out onto the land, the sun warm on our backs. Smelling pine all around us we watched swans circling in a large pond on the property.

The Reverend came out to greet us, a dimple cheeked Santa Claus looking gentleman with dancing blue eyes. We walked around some more, talking about marriage and the seriousness of the commitment.

When he felt assured and comfortable that we were confident in our decision, he led us to a small cemetery on the property. There was an old log building and about a hundred gravestones.

At first, I didn't like the idea of marrying in a cemetery. Isn't marriage hard enough when you begin it together in a church?

Before I could protest, the Reverend began to explain that for him, as a minister, the cemetery is symbolic of a pulpit. Caskets are laid on a church's pulpit before they come to the grave site for final rest. He had married more people in that cemetery than he had buried, so he felt it was his pulpit.

That was good enough for us, so we turned to one another, nervous and touched, and the Reverend began our wedding vows. He turned to me first.

"You will be joining his family; can you do that?"

I said I could, but in hindsight it was rough...

He turned to Joey. "In sickness, Joe. Can you do sickness?" Joey looked into my eyes. "Yeah, I can."

We both began to laugh, as a black and white shepherd pup began playing soccer at our feet, weaving the ball in and around our legs.

"I feel the presence of the Holy Spirit," the Reverend said, his eyes twinkling. Peace descended upon us, and we nodded, dumbstruck with emotion.

"I now pronounce you man and wife. Joe, you may kiss the bride."

We kissed, the sun shone, and we both knew that the Father was present and smiling. As birds flew up and surrounded us, we could barely look at one another, we were so overcome. It was a weepy wedding.

When the heart weeps for what it has lost, the spirit laughs for what it has found.

Sufi teaching

TWO

There are some mornings when you awaken with a sense that a seismic shift in your world is about to occur. My sensing radar is usually correct, and shortly thereafter life comes around and proceeds to kick me a new one. Yesterday, when I woke with a sense of doom that had been building throughout the week, I kept talking to the Lord about trusting Him. I showered and drove to meet Joey, at ten thirty, at the Big R parking lot. He came right on time from work, ran into the convenience store for a quick change of clothes, and walked out looking so handsome he took my breath. For a moment, all was forgotten but his tan skin, wavy brown hair and green eyes. Over the year we have been married, I suddenly find myself with moments of falling in love, and a quickening of my heart which was at first so strangely quiet. Joey is becoming engraved there, more deeply and profoundly than I ever thought possible.

We drove to Colorado Springs, sipping our tea and water respectively, trying to stay positive. We were heading for a new clinic, new doctors, new equipment and hopefully new answers. You see, I have fought chronic illness for over twenty years.

It began while I was working my way back from detox, to what I hoped would be a whole new life. I was riding my bike over a small hill one morning, singing to my heart's content. I encountered, on the other side of that hill, a large white truck with a tank on the back, and two men dressed in zip-up suits and hats with flaps and masks.

They were spraying the trees with big plumes of fluid; before I had time to even close my mouth, the fluid came cascading down on me. That one moment changed my entire life. As I write, I see the entire episode in slow motion: me in my summer shorts, white shirt and dark hair, turning to see one of the men's eyes through the mask he wore, as I yelled, and his look of dismay as he shut off the sprayer…I took off as fast as I could, legs burning, body aching, nervous system movements like the creepy crawls I got as a kid when I thought something was crawling on my skin (but when I reach there's nothing there)…I raced home on my bike, through the ritzy neighborhood alive with the sounds of children playing and gardeners mowing, and inside I'm trembling and cold, and a voice is shouting *take a shower, HURRY!*

So I did, praying to a yet unknown God to help me. That was the beginning for this young girl: a seismic movement. I lost my health, my immune system plummeted, and I began the nightmare of what medicine now affectionately calls "a universal reactor." In other words, the world as we know it, with its modern antibiotics, perfumes, herbicides, petro products (gasoline, asphalt), fresh paint, new carpet, air "fresheners," cigarette smoke and cleaning products…everything designed to make life easier and more attractive, was attacking my body. I couldn't eat, sleep, walk or breathe without pain, the kind of pain that shuts out any hope of living a normal life. In fact, to make a long story short, I ended up living a bit like the character in the John Travolta movie "The Boy In the Plastic Bubble," a film I had seen ten years prior, and had been so profoundly moved that I wept on and off every time I thought about it afterwards. Perhaps we really do have premonitions of things to come.

Instead of a bubble, I lived in an isolation "unit" with other patients who were environmentally ill. We breathed oxygen and filtered air, were attended to by gowned, sometimes masked nurses, and were guinea pigged: brought weak and emaciated to a testing chamber where, blindfolded and nose clipped, we were shut behind thick doors and experimented on, using one chemical or another, and sometimes nothing at all. Sometimes we were tube fed an unknown food or chemical, then observed for reactions, like one would observe mice or rats in a lab. When we began to manifest symptoms (which we almost always did), they would ask for a rating.

If you're gasping for air, no support is offered.

Just rate the symptom, is this a six?

Seeing the head shake. *No? Higher? An eight?*

Ok, an eight then, just to get them to stop staring at you. Once satisfied, they would leave you to suffer alone; unless , of course, a crash cart was needed for a code blue...or an injection was given (as in my case) to knock you into another place, one without form or memory. Tubes were then provided to sustain life, until they could figure out what to do with you.

Me? As usual, I fell through the normal cracks of protocol. I lay in that bed longer than the hostages were held in Iran. When they came home to parades and book and movie offers, I wept, because I had thought, if they can do it I can do it. They did it for over four hundred days. I did it for nearly five years.

I was released from that unit without much hope. My mother and I left immediately on an airplane, bound for yet another hospital and a doctor in Illinois. I was tiny, all sticks and bones with deep dark wounded eyes. I know that through those eyes, I viewed the world with fear. I used to love plane trips. Now they were fraught with danger. Cleaning chemicals, perfume, hairspray, cigarette smoke, fuel fumes, people flying with colds and flu. My lungs tightened, and I strained to breathe with oxygen the entire trip. Amidst stares from my fellow man, we struggled with suitcases to a waiting van. After being in the unit for so long, I enjoyed the open window. The Illinois air was heavy, and I actually found that I was breathing better. We rode quietly, each absorbed in our own thoughts. Mom and Dad had brought me here, using every resource they had. The doctor was expensive, and not covered by insurance. They had done this for me throughout much of my twenty years, as we struggled together to find answers to my body's puzzle.

So we entered another hospital. This time, as the doors locked behind us, the people we shared space with were locked in another kind of world. Once, in Mexico (when I was still a kid drinking milk and eating bread) I stood outside a large windowed building with twenty or thirty others, watching the people inside rock back and forth, hitting the air, dancing crazy dances, and slithering on the floor. I was simultaneously horrified and fascinated.

Loco, loco some kids yelled, and we all moved away from the windows. I took one last look at a boy who peered at me, his tongue darting in and out of his mouth like a snake's.

Loco, I thought. *Crazy.*

Now here I was in a place like that, with people who cried out and hit themselves, who screamed and peed their pants, who dressed up like Tinkerbell and fought invisible foes.

My mom settled me into bed and an I.V. was put in. We spent a week there, having blood tests run, trying to hold onto sanity as all those around me relinquished theirs.

We left the hospital with some answers, and still more questions, getting closer and closer to finding the "One" who could really save us.

A man who believes in nothing but himself lives in a very small world.

Unknown

THREE

It is 1978, and I am preparing to perform before a crowd of five hundred people. It is the season of high boots and flowing skirts, bangles like a gypsy on my wrist, my hair long and flowing. The band is out doing sound check and I am reflecting in the window overlooking the crowd. I light another cigarette and guzzle another vodka and orange juice, and feel the familiar warmth of the liquor coursing through my veins. I am relaxed and smiling, surrounded by onlookers and groupies of the band. They want to capture my attention, and I'm playing "the artist."

The bouncer comes in, our eyes meet in the glass. "Let's go," he says. I turn, eyes cast down, as the band strikes the first riff of "Shoot to Kill." I walk into the crowd without them knowing it. They are fixated on the band, settling in, looking around. Suddenly someone sees me and a hush falls. I cannot look into their faces, but I feel their desire, it pulses into my heart as steadily as the drumbeat.

When I hit the stage, I am ready.

The crowd's noise rises with their bodies as I belt out the first few lines. I finally sense their approval and turn my eyes on them; I feel alive. The alcohol has burned through; now it is just me, given the power to take a heart and let it soar.

It is a feeling I love, a feeling I live for between each show, living on a bus or in a plane, hotels and dive motels, drivers and junk food and people's constant need…I live for that one moment onstage, when the fire connects, and strangers are friends, and I can "…forget about life for a while."

For as long as I can remember, from the time I was a tiny child, I loved to sing and entertain people. There was a time my brother had been very sick in the hospital with asthma, and being so young I was not allowed into the children's ward where he lay. For a week I sat on the long vinyl couch, my feet not touching the ground (sometimes they still don't), watching my parents, doctors and nurses disappear behind a closed door. I'm sure that I had books to read and things to do, but I truly remember being fixated only on that door and what was behind it, my brother.

One day, my parents came out with some doctors, and told me that they were going down to another floor to talk with still another doctor… after assuring me that they would be back, they disappeared from sight. I got an idea going in my head, and my heart began to pound. I decided to go and find my brother. I slid off the couch, and walked quickly through the door, keeping my eyes focused on one thing: finding Brett!

I ran from room to room, peeking in, seeing one very sick child after another. Just as I was despairing of ever finding him I turned a corner into a room and there he lay. He was under an oxygen tent, pale as the sheet over him, eyes closed, lips blue. I was frightened, so frightened I began to tremble. Just then he turned and opened his eyes. The eyes that focused on me were not the eyes of my brother, yet there he lay.

This scared me further, and in my fear I found myself moving in a strange clownlike manner, singing softly. I moved closer to his crib, and kept dancing, until finally he smiled at me. My God, what a smile…my heart sang and my legs moved, and I danced and sang on, oblivious to my surroundings, until a firm hand and a stern and startled voice broke my concentration.

"What are you *doing* ?" snapped Nurse Ratchet. "*Children* are not allowed in here!"

I looked at my brother frantically and found that he had retreated back behind his closed eyes.

"Let's *go*, young lady!"

Ratchet had a hold of me and was pushing me out of the ward, back down the hall, and through that door, where she pushed me down onto the vinyl couch.

"You sit here and do *not* move!" she hissed, as she made her way back through the door. I sat there reeling from shock and fear. Then suddenly, I realized that I had made my brother smile. In the worst of all possible situations, my clowning and singing had pulled him out of his pain. I was suddenly sharply aware of the power of that, and I was hooked. It was all I wanted to do: sing and dance and make people forget about pain for a while.

But the concert is over now, and I crash down within me as they swarm for my attention.

"Will you sign my shirt?" they ask. "Can I speak to you?" A reporter follows me backstage. "Can I come in?"

I feel sheer panic inside me. The outpouring of my soul is past and I have nothing left to give them. "I'm sorry," I mumble as I shut the stage door, "Not now."

I reach for my purse, and swallow the little yellow pill which, for the past five years, has been my constant friend. I light a cigarette and wait for the calm after the storm. When it finally comes, I smooth my hair and open the door.

A small crowd still lingers, and as I walk towards the bus and the band I am smiling. Some of them look at me, and others follow. I hug this time, and flirt, and sail on the wings of a drug, because my own wings have yet to spread... to the next show, the next high, the next stroke of midnight, when Cinderella turns back into the peasant girl, holding the slipper, wishing for the pain to go away.

We carry within us the wonders we seek without us.

Sir Thomas Brown

FOUR

This morning the land was bathed in a pink and wheat glow, and the air was completely still. I threw on my old gray sweats and opened the screen door. The sky was blue, like a robin's egg, a color truly only found as God mixes the paint. Miss B, our magnificent seventy five pound greyhound, comes up to greet me, her soft brown eyes excited that I am up and our walk is imminent.

When the land is awakened in such splendor, when the air is thick with the fragrances of wildflowers, I find no greater place than to go into the early morning light and draw deeply into my lungs and spirit, God. It is here that I find God so real, so tangible.

His hand is everywhere, in every creature as small as the insect that lands on my hand and washes its face with tiny wings; or in the cry of coyote pups in the dark night, under a blanket of stars that takes my breath away…so immense, that I feel lost, and in the same moment, found.

Our mountains wrap around the western view of the property, and change moods often throughout the day. Sometimes they are shrouded in fluffy white clouds that lay thick upon them to keep them warm. Other times, shadows of the sun lazily caress the curves of canyons, moving across in washes of color. It is from over the mountains that the storms come: deep, dense, ripe with rain and sharp barbs of lightening that randomly strike to rumbling, booming, earth shaking thunder. We quiver, Miss B and I, and occasionally a near strike will find us huddled together seeking comfort and shelter, our limbs shaking together, waiting for the fury to subside.

I survived a lightening hit years before, and still live with the reminders in my heart, which beats erratically under stress. The land humbles me, a mere mortal bestowed with her gift of glory… a caretaker, mistress and slave am I to her power, her moods, her beauty. It is here that I know of God's awesome power, as He said to Job 38:34-35:

Can you raise your voice to the clouds and cover yourself with a flood of water? Do you send the lightening bolts on their way? Do they report to you "Here we are" ?

If the land moves me so, how much greater the Creator of the land!

God, in His amazing, all powerful completeness, so unfathomable to me, lays through my heart in a mysterious relationship with His Son, Jesus, and uses this land to teach me a tiny bit more about myself and Him. Here, humbled, I can only return time and time again to His spirit, which whispers in the wind, moves in raging storms, and speaks softly to me of His Love.

> **Life is difficult and good.**
>
> *Frank Lee*

FIVE

I am waiting, as I usually do, for evening to come and for the dark to create a need for the warmth of our little trailer. I can hear them working in the house, made from bricks of dirt from our own land. I can see the house from the trailer, and it is becoming, before my very eyes, a home. I will call it The House That Love Built, because my dad the architect designed it, my husband is building it, my mom is supporting it, and I am praying for it. Then there are all the people who have become like family, contributing their time and skills. We sit in the sun and eat our lunches, laugh at one another's escapades, and share vitamins as often as we have shared colds. Some would say they are employees and we are the bosses, but I believe strongly that this house is also theirs, because they raised it up. This new baby will be ours, but they were a big part of the conception. I, of all of us, have had the least to do with this child that is being birthed for me. I feel a little like an expectant parent, impatient and longing to be able to take possession. But really the house will only be mine for a season in life, and I want to share it as often as we are able. So I wait, for the saw noises to subside, for the trucks to pull away, and for Joey to come home, dirty with saw dust and smiling at the smell of chicken soup, and because I will crawl into our tiny shower with him to wash his back. It's a nightly ritual to engage closeness after a day apart. The workers leave as the sun settles into its pink glory. Miss B sits, watching all the activity of the day wind down. I am waiting for Joey, and the phone rings. It is my friend and confidant Vicky, God's gift of friendship and sisterhood. She is sick with food poisoning, and is calling to let us know that they will be unable to come spend Valentine's weekend with us, because her husband has to go to school. But "she would love to come and spend my birthday with me."

So we make our arrangements. As I hang up I am reminded once again about the treasures of life. They are nothing more than the love of a lifelong friendship, the love of family, and the love of a man who took my hand for better or for worse and meant it.

We found a tiny country church and took communion. One moment we are in the Spirit, the next we are in our flesh. How do I know the difference? Because the Spirit is full of love and power, mercy and grace. And our flesh? Angry frustrated words and the slamming of doors. Marriage is certainly a mirror. Interdependent are we, so much so that when one is acting like a baby, the other climbs right into the crib as well.

"Mine!" the child yells. "No me!" the other cries. Is it not so?

Joey walks through the door and I read him this page. We laugh.

"Isn't that the truth? Babies…"

"In grownup bodies," I counter. We hold each other close. It is good to be able to talk things through. I see so clearly my broken places. I know that life has left some deep cracks, some chips and even a few pieces missing. I know so clearly that all the years of running from myself and my circumstances, used and abused by many, hurting myself with alcohol and drugs and sex, always feeling totally alone, that there had to be something better. I pondered about this Higher Power, this God, that as a child I had once desired to know.

For years and years, God was a religion, a God of "don'ts," a God I feared.

Now I know that God is my Daddy, my friend, my healer. He speaks to me in the solitude of my heart. When I met God, I fell in love with Him, and I could never leave Him again. Certainly God and I have been through times of anger, hurt, and bewilderment.

The really wonderful part about a relationship so full of love and power is that the other party (GOD) can take my anger, help me with my misunderstandings, hold me when I'm hurting, and give prompt attention when I'm bewildered. God, is the same yesterday, today, and forevermore. I am the mercurial barometer of mood and temperament, shifting, squirming, controlling, manipulating, struggling, releasing, relaxing, tensing, frustrated and finally submitting, relinquishing, becoming soft and safe as I enter into God's presence.

I believe Jesus said it best, when in the Garden, the night before He allowed them to take Him away to His death, when He knew that His purpose for mankind was unfolding, and that He would carry the load that no man could bear (the sins of this world), He fought within Himself in agony, in His humanness.

Father, if it is possible for You to take this cup away from Me, please do…but (releasing, relinquishing, dying to self) not My will, but Thy will be done.

So Jesus went forth, and hung naked on a Cross until He died. After three days He rose again from the dead. I know this seems impossible, but that is what makes this so real, and so different from any other great man of God: Jesus lives! Five hundred people saw Him alive after He was crucified…and one man, named Thomas (Doubting Thomas) even got to place his fingers in the holes where the nails had been driven, because he didn't believe his eyes.

More importantly, my belief in God went from religion to relationship when I asked Jesus to come live in me, in my heart, and change me.

I did, He did… and love came to stay.

Yet my struggle to change character still involves a daily understanding that, moment by moment, I can only have the "garden experience" that Christ had when He said "NOT my will, but Thine be done." I can still become that other girl: the one so easily lost to sin. My sins may have changed from alcohol, drugs, sex and selfishness, to a sharp tongue or a controlling action, but the very character of me still remains. Paul said it best when he said, "The very thing I *don't* want to do is what I will do." What has changed for me is my desire. My deepest place within me wants to change, and wants to do what God wants me to do, not what I want to do. I know that many people reject Christ because of Christians. The world expects us to be different. I believe that our hearts desire to be perfect, but our wounded selves need healing. As Christians we can only confess our lack and wait for Jesus to act.

I recently saw a bumper sticker that said, "Please be patient, God isn't through with me yet."

Either life is a grand adventure or a desperate enduring.

Unknown

SIX

Life has a peculiar way of changing directions when you least expect it. I've heard the expression, "Life is what happens when you're making other plans." I say, "God is what happens when you're making other plans."

I remember once I planted a garden from seed, and I couldn't remember where I had planted what, so I had to wait for the plants to come up. I was amazed at what came up where; I could have sworn those carrots were somewhere else. So either I mixed the seeds up, or God played a funny on me. I've always thought that anyone who created the aardvark or insects that I've seen must have a practical joker kind of humor. Is it presumptuous of me to think of God that way? I think not, for as I expressed earlier, God and Jesus and The Holy Spirit are my number one relationships in life. This relationship is real: real emotions, real joy, real amazement and laughter. God and I talk, a lot. He is usually my first conversation of the day.

So when life throws me a curve ball, and I seem to strike out and have to sit on the bench, I know that God is in the midst of things, a great coach, teaching His cocky, independent player a lesson.

The other day I woke in a great deal of pain, my blue down comforter felt heavy; to rise and make my way into the morning sun seemed a grand effort and I found, to my dismay, that I could *not* get enough air. The muscles in my neck, back and chest were rigid. I felt as if someone had their hands around my neck and was choking me. I of course went immediately to prayer, and as the hours passed without relief, I felt panic arise. I felt that I was about to die. At that moment I suddenly felt my spirit stand up strong within my bent and rigid body, and as the tears poured down my cheeks, through wheezes and gasps for air, I began to praise Him. I praised Him for His love, His mercy, my family, my friends, my husband, our land. I praised Him and I praised Him. I love my Daddy, my Father God; I am learning to trust Him, no matter what. The day got worse; what we discovered was that some of the building materials brought to frame our home had been treated in chemicals that were hurting me. Joey and my father had brought them onto my safe and comforting land.

"You're supposed to *protect* me!" I cried out in fear. "I don't know about building materials!"

Gasping for air, I got into the car and drove away, speeding through the countryside as I'd had to so many times in the city, running away from a chemical that was hurting me. I saw Joey's tight face and angry set mouth, and I heard the pain in my father's voice. I heard Joey yell, "We have no other choice, if you want your house built!"

"Figure something else out!" I gasped out as I drove away. The pain in my chest was immense, but as I drove up the mountain and breathed cleaner air, the symptoms began to subside. I struggled to understand how two people who loved me so very much could be so careless with my health. They both admitted knowing that the materials soaked in the chemical stank beyond belief! I struggle with all the pain this disease brings, not only to me, but to those I love.

As I watched the moon rise into the starry sky, I searched my heart to forgive those who don't mean to hurt me but do. I searched my heart to forgive myself for being sick, and a burden to those I love. I do so love my dear family, and I want to live long years close to them. I know that too many more exposures like that one could kill me.

The cool night air blew against my cheek, as I took my first deep breath of the day. "Lord, running from the air is such a hideous way to live. Heal me, oh God. You alone, only You, can heal me. No doctor can heal me. Even this land won't be able to heal me, as I know You intended, if people bring in the wrong things."

I drove back down the mountain through the dark, and saw my husband take off in the truck with the toxic frames. I could tell by the way he was driving that he was angry. I came back to our precious land and was finally able to breathe again. Walking like an old woman, I took off my clothes and climbed into our hot tub under the stars, and I prayed: for Joey, for Dad, for the builders, for the land, and for all people everywhere who suffer torment because the air they breathe is toxic. They suffer without understanding: depression, unexplainable rage, headaches, muscle aches, fatigue, coughing, diarrhea, asthma, sore throats, watery eyes. Just about every symptom known to man can be attributed to the air we breathe. As man continues to pollute with pesticides, herbicides, asphalt, petro chemicals, nerve gas, paint, carpet, formaldehyde, etc; more and more people will be struck down with debilitating and often fatal diseases. And they won't know what hit them.

A thing of beauty is a joy forever.

John Keats

SEVEN

The studio lights in the photographer's loft were still cold when I came through the door, no makeup, sweats and wet hair. It was up to the dynamic trio to make the magic happen. The dynamic trio was comprised of JB, the hairstylist; Jen, the makeup artist; and Randy, the photographer. A model is truly the least part of the illusion you see in print. We never look like the picture you see.

I was up for a jeans spot; a talent search for "The Great American Butt." I was primped, pumped and glossed, then perched on corral fences, pickup trucks and fields of flowers. Modeling was fun; I was queen for a day. I found it was always hard to go home and do the dishes afterwards. During the years I was pursuing my dreams for stardom and fame, through the still lens, the paintbrush, voice, TV or movie camera, a subtle shift in thinking began to manifest. I was only ok as long as I was pleasing to someone. The record producer or the agent, the movie man or the photographer…"Beautiful, sexy, hot!" the photographer would say, and I felt that way then, as long as he thought so. "I wish you were taller," the agent says. "I wish you were blonde. We need a blonde."

"I can do blonde," I'd say, and head for the nearest Clairol bottle.

"Wow!" the movie moguls from Japan said. "You're an actress! Sign here, report to location on Monday." So I did. I was a prostitute in a prison cell, spouting anger, vulnerability and fear. I could do that easily; it was me. The movie released in Japan, and then on the big screen in America.

21

I was on television for a season, hosting a talk show. I recorded an album of gospel music; there was talk of touring. My paintings were in galleries. I was interviewed by newspapers.

I am somebody as long as somebody wants me, is interested, pursues.

According to an article in a Denver newspaper I am "Someone to watch."

Now, twelve years and many traumas later, nearing forty three years of age, silver in my hair, wrinkles on my face, brought back to the land isolated and lonely, I seek my identity once again. The world says I am too old, too short, too gray, too wrinkled. My body isn't the buff creation it once was after hours a day at the gym. Some days I agree with the world's assessment: washed up, tired and old. My disease speaks to me about such matters, and I confess I often listen. When I listen, life hurts.

But when I listen to God's view of me, that I am valuable to Him, precious and dearly loved…when I allow that truth to sink in, life can have meaning and purpose, and even joy. It is a simple statement, yet for someone whose whole life has been about doing, about being, about striving to be enough, it is not easily incorporated into my soul.

It is a daily decision, that when thoughts come to "steal, kill and destroy me," I have to make the effort to say "No."

If anyone is in Christ, he is a new creation; the old has gone, the new has come.

As I grow older, as I take the road chosen, I am learning the secret to life is "not what happens to you, but how you *respond* to what happens to you." Fight it and it gets harder; release and accept it, and trust God with it…and God will be God. For God's love is not conditional on my accomplishments, my beauty, the amount of money I have or the response of people towards me.

God's love is so great that He gave His only begotten Son, Jesus, that whosoever believeth in Him shall have everlasting life.

If I were the only person left on the face of this earth Jesus would still give His life for me, as He has given His life for you, and within that precious truth I find I will always be beautiful to those that matter most: those who see me through the eyes of love.

> ***The only way around is through.***
>
> ***Robert Frost***

EIGHT

The heat of the sun pounded upon my bare shoulders. Joey and I stood facing one another as the wind whipped my hair. The sky that Indian summer day was blue, and Joey's eyes looked startled, like a deer caught in the headlights, when I approached him. Between my sickness and building the house, we hadn't heated up the blankets for a long time. Suddenly my husband looked sexy, and I became acutely aware of the way his hair was golden and his muscled arm was brown.

"How bout a dance?" I whispered, kissing his neck. He took me to him, and we began to two step on the land, twirling and back, rocking our hips together, throwing our heads back and laughing. Suddenly I saw our life as if we were in a movie: my dress with lace underclothes, his body poured into tight black jeans, my hand moving on his chest and back, muscled and moist with sweat as we danced. Allowing myself to move into the sweetness of the moment, I am on the verge of a memory, a moment of sensations from my childhood, when each night tucked into bed I could feel safe, and each morning was a new day anticipating greatness, like hitting a home run, or running to school and never feeling afraid. This childhood memory all came before another seismic movement in time.

At age seven, all alone, four high school boys, on the grounds of a church, covered my face, pulled down my pants, and took what was never theirs to begin with: a little girl's safety and trust and honesty and openness.

Suddenly, remembering the pain, an invisible door comes to slam out the laughter, the openness, the desire. I stop dancing with Joey and feel myself withdraw, back into a more controlled emotion. No more play. "I'll fix lunch, are you hungry?" I ask. "For you," he says. What was once sweetness and love has become a woman's chore. I love him. He is still sexy and loving, and I feel numb, like you get when ice has sat too long on your skin. He often knows when my moods change, but today I am determined to hide it from him. He deserves a fully functional woman. *God*, I pray. *Let me give.*

Marriage brings memories to the surface. Perhaps at last, in the safety of Joey's loving arms, every hidden pain, like an abscess, will begin to come out. If we don't lance the thing and get the putrid poisons out, nothing can heal. I want to heal. I want the memories to leave… a female baby sitter who tied me to a bed and raped me with a broom handle to punish me. All the lessons in betrayal, first love to last, the cheating, the lying, diseases, the modeling years of *sex sells*. A man who enters my home and calls me names too evil to write about as he rapes me, taking from me any healing that may have been gained from remembering. Men who threatened and controlled, a baby conceived in emotional abuse and physical intimidation…lost months later in an operating room as my life ebbed away. Sex has hurt me, shook any hope of purity or goodness. Healing has yet to come.

But perhaps with time, Joey, true and faithful, loving and patient, with his love and our prayers, will help me begin the process of letting these memories go. Surely God in His mercy will heal the rest.

When we pray to God we must be seeking nothing.

Francis of Assisi

NINE

I have been in a faith crisis for the last few days. Joey and I have been nightly reading a book by the late Katharine Kuhlman, a woman used mightily by God. Through her ministry many people were healed.

Every night for weeks we have been reading one case history after another of people being healed. Some had great faith, some seemed to have no faith at all. They all did have one thing in common: all were desperate. I have been feeling very under the weather for weeks now, and trying to keep the faith, but God has seemed distant to us lately.

Anyway, in the last few weeks I found out a little girl who I love and who had accepted Christ with me one night, has spinal meningitis and was in a coma. She is now coming back, but has to re-learn everything. I've been in the hospital for my heart; Vicky, my best friend, has been in the hospital for her stomach; then last night I read in *Life Magazine*, the incredibly sad story of a young girl, who at age thirteen, developed a disease that shut her digestion down. She spent years in her room, her mother injecting her thirty times a day just to keep her alive, as she waited for an organ donor to become available. She watched the world go by through her window, isolated and suffering. Her faith was strong; they prayed and read Scripture daily. When the call came after four years, she wrote in her diary thanking the Lord that finally she could be healthy and live a normal life that she so desperately wanted. She made it through all the pain of the transplant, and on the fourth day ate French fries. Days later she began to fail, and then she died. Her mother, a strong believer, says that it rocked her soul. She doesn't kill herself only because she is afraid she that she won't be able to see her precious daughter in heaven. I found myself crying after I read the story, and could not quit. A profound sorrow overcame me, and then a steady flickering of fear and anger. Joey came home to find me crying.

"What's wrong, honey?" he asked, and I began to cry louder.

"I'm having a crisis about God. We've been reading about a God who healed people randomly, without faith, with faith, a God who made dying people whole. But what about the people He doesn't heal? The ones like this little girl who died? She had great faith, she loved Jesus.

Lots of people were praying and believing , and she suffered and died!" I'm inconsolable now, acutely aware that I am crossing some invisible line. " Like me! Where is God concerning me? Why are we even building this house for me if I'm going to suffer and die?"

I feel as if I have melted into a substance without form or support, melting with fear and anxiety and anger. "We've been praying!

Believing, seeking, and has God moved towards us? Has He? Do you feel Him or hear from Him?"

Joey was trying to hold onto me. "No," he said in his quiet way. "But we have to keep believing."

I sit feeling guilt and anguish for having spoken those words. But it is true. The question has come, inconsolable, and there is no answer.

How do you carry on for twenty years, kept alive but never healed?

How do you have one near death experience after another, snatched from the jaws of death time and time again, delivered by degrees from pain and suffering so deep; moving into some semblance of a life with promise and hope, only to have your dreams taken again by a disease that threatens endless suffering and death?

In that stark reality, how do I continue to have faith in a God who says that we have infinite power in His name; we have healing and deliverance and His never ending love? Then where is it?

That is my pain this day: trying to understand that through it all God is in control, that He still loves me and that He is still ultimately good.

*The reason angels can fly is because they take themselves so
lightly.*

G.K. Chesterton

TEN

The land was shaken the next morning with wind. The grove
of oak trees, which through the summer had stood calm and
serene, were now bending and shaking. Dust was raised, and
when Miss B and I went out for our walk it was difficult to stand
upright. Miss B's ears were flapping and my hair whipped my
face, stinging my eyes. My mom and dad came up in a large
truck, bringing more bricks for the foundation of our adobe
house in progress. I had gone over to the truck to bring out
packages and suitcases, and was walking through the foundation
and septic area of the construction site, when I twisted my ankle
and fell hard to the earth. I cried out, and Joey came and carried
me over to a bench by the trailer.

"I'm ok," I said, smiling. "Save your strength, Bub, for all
those cement bricks."

The ankle began to swell, and by evening I couldn't walk. It
was black and blue and definitely painful. This, after a day of
water tanks and trucks breaking down, and workers not showing
up; basically a *day*, if you grasp my meaning.

I crawled up to bed with ice on my foot and began to read.
What in the world was God trying to teach me?

I moved my foot and groaned as the phone rang. It was
Vicky calling from Denver. We caught up, and she asked if she
could pray for my foot. "Sure," I said halfheartedly (I have
shared with you about my current state of faith).

Her prayer was beautiful and heartfelt, and I sensed that God
was doing something. He did. By evening's end, I could bend
my toes and walk on it. The swelling was down and the pain was

abating. I went to God in prayer after Joey was softly snoring. I prayed in tongues, that remarkable gift given to me years before. As I listened to the lyrically beautiful utterances from my soul, I asked God for interpretation. It came in the form of a silent voice in my spirit, that I have come to sense as God's.

I am God and there is no other.

I lay in the dark, reflecting on the past few days. My despair and heartache for that little girl who had faith and died, the constant harassing problems of broken trucks, a broken TV, another broken windshield, the windstorms, the hurting body, the touch of God to heal my foot while other things stay unchanged...

I am God. There is no other.

I am reminded of Scripture that says, *He sends rain to fall on the wicked and the righteous alike.*

I lie there recognizing that God has come this night to make it clear to me that He *does* hear our prayers, and He is the One who chooses to answer. Sometimes the answer is not what we want, sometimes the answer is long in coming. Sometimes we get our heart's desire.

Tonight, He moved to heal my foot, to let me know once again that He alone is the Healer. He chooses to heal, He moves when He chooses, and we must learn to accept that in our pain, our darkness and our confusion...God is not silent. He is working.

For He is God, and there is no other.

When you're going through hell, keep going…

Winston Churchill

ELEVEN

Joey and I fought. It was a fight that came out of nowhere, picked from the dark recesses of our minds, like a silent shadow ready to strike. We had driven to Denver together at daybreak. He was taking me to the doctor, then we planned to go antique shopping. The day had been city driven; by that I mean we had to deal with traffic jams and car accidents, police sirens and people with attitudes. We sat an hour in traffic and went three miles. We were late and had headaches.

The sky stayed gray and heavy, and there was no sun. We walked through stores and I kept having to find a bathroom. I felt sick and achy, tired and cross. Ten hours later, driving the one hundred and forty two miles home, he said something, I said something, he said something else.

The something else triggered a memory. It was from deep within me, of a night twelve years before…when a stranger came into my house.

He played nice for a while, and when it became obvious that I needed him to leave, he turned evil. The *evil* called me names as he slammed my body down to the old wooden floor and raped me from behind. He kept me to the floor and I was aware of a voice inside me that said to stop fighting. The *evil* was six foot two inches tall and a body builder.

I stand five feet two on a good day and ninety eight pounds soaking wet. I stopped struggling as he grabbed my hair, yanked my head back and began kissing my neck.

That's better, he said. *Just take it.*

I did. I went to the Lord, I saw Him on the cross…taking it.

When the *evil* was through, I crawled to the bathroom, turned on the shower and crept into the steaming hot curtain of water. He followed me in and sat on the commode, talking about his mother, who he hated; the women who hurt him, his need to stop their actions towards him. He began to talk about a young girlfriend who had betrayed him, and said how "they had found her dead." My breath stopped in my chest and the pounding of my heart increased. *My God*, I thought. *He's going to kill me.* I was shaking, the kind of uncontrollable shaking that a body does when the mind screams *run* and you cannot. You just sit paralyzed as the water runs cold, and *evil's* voice escalates into hysteria.

"I'm sorry," I heard a voice say, and realized it was mine. "I'm sorry all those women hurt you…but I know someone who will never hurt you…or leave you."

"Who?" he snarled.

"Jesus," I said. "Jesus Christ."

I sat waiting behind the shower curtain, shaking, yet suddenly remarkably calm. The evil voice dropped and I realized that he was crying. His voice became that of a young boy. "I don't want to be bad," he said. "I just want to be loved."

"Jesus loves you," I whispered. "He will never leave you, and He will forgive you," I said more boldly. The curtain suddenly parted and he was holding a towel. "Come on," he said. "Get out so we can go to bed."

Oh God no, he's not staying! I want him to leave…please God make him leave…

But he didn't leave. He took me to my bedroom and pulled the mattress off the bed, and put it on the floor. He crawled under the covers and pulled me down next to him.

"I'm tired," he said. "Really tired."

I lay next to him, tears falling down my cheeks, my body in a state of alert, waiting, waiting for what? The *evil* to awaken and want my body again? Or for dawn to break, or for me to make a move and get out?

After a time, I began to move my legs, inching them towards the edge of the bed, heavy, aching, could they really be my legs? I began to slide out from the sheets when he snatched my arm.

"Where are you going?" he inquired, the voice low.

"Nowhere," I said. *Nowhere.*

I lay beside him listening to the night and never moved again. When daybreak came, he got up and took a shower. I lay there. He came back into the room and looked at me.

"I have to go to work," he said. "Walk me to the door."

My heart began to pound again. Was he really leaving?

"OK," I said, trying to keep my voice even. "Let me get my robe."

I threw the robe over my aching body as he watched me. We walked out through the bedroom, the hallway and past the living room where it had all happened. *Evil* turned to me and kissed me. *I love you*, he said. I forced a smile and opened the door. He stood for a second and then walked out. I slammed the door and locked it, and slid down the length of the door to the floor, weeping, softly sobbing, *Thank God he's gone, thank God he's gone.* Thank God the dawn had come and I was alive. "Jesus," I cried out. "Oh Jesus…"

If that had been all of it, I would have thought it too much. But now the *evil* in the man had heard the name of Jesus. His agenda, which I believe had been to kill me, had been aborted, and now the man within the evil had felt the touch of Christ. He was drawn to the love of God, and knew only of me. He began to call, between ten and eighteen times a day. I never answered personally, just sat in the room and let the machine pick it up. I parked my car blocks away from my front door. I never opened the windows, curtains or doors. I got a roommate, who was appalled at the phone calls. I saw him, stalking me on more than one occasion, and left through back doors while he inquired at the front. I never went to the police, but called and politely inquired if I had any legal way to stop this man. A restraining order could be put in motion, but I feared it would set him off. I preferred to hide instead.

Six weeks later, I was stopped in traffic by a police officer. He leaned into the window and smiled.

"I'm single," he said. "Are you?" He was young, strong and charming.

"Yes…"

"Instead of a ticket for speeding, how about lunch?" He was smiling, clearly nervous.

A policeman, a badge, a uniform, protection. "OK." I smiled shyly.

We went to an open park with a sack lunch and talked. He seemed kind and very interested. After we had dated for six weeks, I told him about the *evil*.

"Don't worry, honey. I'll take care of it."

True to his words, a few days later the phone calls stopped. For the first time in months I began to feel safe. A year later, we married, on a fall day in a mansion in the country, and later still it became clear we had married for all the wrong reasons. In three months he had moved out and filed for divorce, in another year it was all over. He wasn't a Christian, or a man who believed in fidelity. Biblically I was free. But the pain sat on my chest like a truck and would not let go. I knew that I needed more healing, more help, more from God. But instead of running to my Savior, I was angry with God for all the pain. So I ran as fast as I could into the arms of the world. It took me the better part of six years to find my way back home. Along the long road back, I found in me a splintered side that could not be made whole no matter how hard I tried. I began pursuing modeling and acting, became a blonde and a gym rat. The fact is, I wanted to be anybody but who I was. I wore life as one would wear clothes. I changed myself, my attitude, my hair color, my home, my boyfriends, my careers; and still I could not find peace or joy or truth. I fought God's ways and yet found myself preaching of His love. I walked a fence and I knew it, but I was a person split in two: I wanted God, but God's ways were hard. I wanted life to be easy, to be fun, to be without pain. The world held me like a small prey in a spider's web. I felt valued when a handsome man turned his attention on me, I felt valued when my art show sold a lot of work, I felt important when I was picked to host a television show, or when I was selected to sing solo before two thousand people. As long as I had all the attention, I could hide my disease, hide the pain I felt every time I was exposed to chemicals. I could fake that. I hurt every single day as if I had the flu, but I could hide my depressions, my fears, my feelings of worthlessness. Living alone enabled me to shut the door, turn off the phone and sleep or watch TV for days until my strength returned.

Only a few people ever saw the real me. What most of the world saw was an impassioned active powerhouse who spent most of her days perfecting her outward appearance and ignoring her spirit and soul.

As beautiful and sexy as I worked to become, I was all tears and rage on the inside. If a man did not do what I wanted, if I could not control him, I would get mad and then cry. No one ever told me that I was out of line or that I needed help. They simply left without a backward glance. I always felt lonely, yet there was always another waiting to take a piece of me, one that I was always willing to give. But I had no concept at that time of the value. Love carries a high price, as does lust, greed and selfishness. So in the frenzy to have more, to get more, to be more…all can be lost.

> **May you live all the days of your life.**
>
> **Jonathan Swift**

TWELVE

The nights on the land are clear and cold with layers of stars. Miss B and I will on occasion take a moonlit walk, while Joey works on finishing some project by lantern light. I am always completely overwhelmed and humbled by the vast ocean of stars. In the city you only get a glimpse of what splendor lies above us. On the land, we are engulfed as if we too are a part of the sky. Without the buildings, the sky touches everywhere. I realize, as I'm standing out under the universe, how truly small I am. When I get to feeling like I'm too big for my britches that's all I have to do: look up, and God puts things in perspective.

Yesterday my late period came. The older I get, the more that monthly time takes over my life. I sometimes have cramps so bad I am doubled over. I have days prior to the bleeding that I feel completely disassociated, depressed and very irritable. Then comes the headache. Yesterday the cramps started first and then the headache. I lay in the trailer (all shades pulled), clutching my head and crying. Joey came home, took one look at me and began massaging my feet, my legs, my back, my neck, praying all the while.

It took an hour to get the pain manageable. I was finally able to open my eyes. Joey was looking at me and smiled. "Better?" he asked.

"Thank you." I breathed a sigh of relief. He leaned towards me, his three day beard scratching my face. "Will you marry me?" he asked. I sort of snorted, because Joey always gets romantic when I feel the least lovable.

"We *are* married, you goof." I find it's warm and safe in his arms.

"Again," he whispers. "Marry me again."

"I have, I will, I do," I say, smiling.

Before I met this man, I had been in a relationship for many years with a handsome man with whom I was madly in love. He lied to me, cheated on me, gave me diseases and left me for another woman. I took him back. When we finally broke up, I was in the hospital and had nearly died. I told him I had gone back to Jesus and couldn't live in sin any more. He left and never returned. Eight months later he married another. Needless to say I was hurt, so I had given up on men, had told God that if He had a man for me, he would have to show up at my door, Bible in one hand and roses in the other, and say out loud that God had sent him. Joey showed up virtually the next day. I met him at my door. I was in a dirty bathrobe and not too pleased to see him. He "aw shucks'd" me with his boyish charm and said he was sorry, he should have called first; he just wondered if I wanted to go to a movie. I looked at him.

"Come in, I've got something to tell you. If you still want to go to the movies afterwards, then we'll go."

I directed him to the couch and sat across from him, looked him straight in the eye, took a deep breath and began. "I'm a tongue speakin', Bible thumpin' woman with a calling from God. I have a chronic illness and I can't have babies." I saw his eyes widen. "So... you still want to go to the movies?" I expected him to say no and run as fast as he could out the door.

Instead he leaned back, smiled at me and said, "Yeah, I do."

"You do?" I was incredulous.

"Yeah, I do."

I looked at him. Something warm was beginning in my chest. He smiled at me and I suddenly knew I was in trouble. We never did make that movie.

We talked six nights running till dawn, went to church together for our first date, and married on the eighth day. Whoever said "God works in mysterious ways" was not kiddin'. I thank God every day for the love I have been given through this man. Some days I feel that between God, Joey, and the land, I will be healed.

The fact that nobody wants to believe something doesn't keep it from being true.

Unknown

THIRTEEN

Joey and I sit in the doctor's office after all the tests have been run. I notice that the tile on the floor is European and expensive. I see that the doctor is reading the papers in front of him with a frown. I look at Joey who smiles at me with soft eyes. I'm feeling a lot of pain in my chest and I'm cold. The doctor looks up and hands me a readout. It shows that my heart, lungs, stomach and bladder are under tremendous stress. There are five stages of the progression of my disease, and I am in the fourth stage. The fifth is death. My immune system appears to be functioning at about thirty percent. The doctor is sorry, but it's important that... I should not expose myself to the clinic environment where I have been in practice any more. I don't have the reserves to fight off the pathogens there.

I begin to cry. It sounds to me like I am dying. The doctor continues to explain that I need to avoid as many exposures as possible, and that it could take five to seven years to heal... if I still have the ability to heal at all.

Years before, after being sent home by the medical establishment to die in suffering and without peace, I began to read about the world of alternative health practices. I went to a chiropractor and an acupuncturist. Within their walls I found some relief from the constant agony my body was sending me. I remember thinking, " Well at least that is something! The other doctors can offer me nothing."

So I began to explore, through books, the incredible world of alternative medicine. I began to understand that we cannot just cover up symptoms (they are after all the body's way of telling us something is wrong), but that we must figure out why we are having the symptoms and remove the cause, then cleanse the body of the poisons that we eat and breathe and drink in every day, so that our cells can begin to do their proper job, and nourish our bodies so they can rebuild.

I loved reading about the world of vitamins and minerals and amino acids, and that our bodies are basically electrical, and need proper nutrients to "fire" so that we can function. I read everything that I could get my hands on, and slowly, over time, perseverance and God's will, I did not die, but found myself growing stronger. Eventually I went back to school, got my naturopathic degree and began to help others as I had been helped. I have yet to be completely healed, but the girl who was sent home to die by traditional medicine is alive twenty one years later. Off and on throughout the years, as my health has allowed, I have had private clients and patients. The doctor we are visiting today knows that I am presently working in a large city clinic.

Joey is looking hard at me and not reacting. I'm not sure that he understands what is being said; the doctor has been speaking to me as one doctor to another.

He is so clinical about it all, and I can't be. This is about me, about my hopes and dreams going up in the drone of his voice. I wish we had never come seeking answers, seeking hope. This is a profound shock, and I can't wait to leave.

Instead I ask, not as a doctor, but as a patient desperate for hope, if I have a chance. The question hangs there as if unheard, and I realize that it is unanswerable.

Only God knew the answer for my life, and He was not audible in the room. He seemed in fact a million years away, as I sat freezing cold, shaky with shock, acutely aware of my own mortality.

It's a moment where you can put a number on all the back pains, the stomach aches, the weight loss, the breathlessness, the fatigue so heavy you carry it around like a lead filled blanket wrapped around your shoulders. Pain which has lived with me is suddenly more than just a "pain". It is a heart, a lung, a stomach or a bladder reaching out for help, and I am out of answers. The doctor in me, the one who has been paid $60.00 an hour to find answers for others, some as desperate as myself, is unable to help. Cool, full of faith and hope for my patients, I reflect on the times I sat across the desk from them, grasping their hands in prayer for God to heal, to use me as a tool… suddenly I find I am a cranky, bored, frightened, restless patient, lying in bed without peace or serenity, fighting worry, angry and sad.

I cry out to God for relief, and He is silent. I lie in my bed, living out on the land without the creature comforts of the infirm. No friends, no T.V., no big tub to soak in. Joey goes off every morning before I wake up, and comes home fourteen to sixteen hours later, ready to sleep. I no longer have an office to go to, no more patients to worry about, no more distractions from myself. It is the hell of sickness, the introspection, the endless hours preoccupied with self. I read the Bible, which was once so alive, and is now mere words on a page. My God who I talk to every morning, walking, seeking answers, is not someone or something I can control. He is my only hope, and for now He is glaringly silent, or strangely firm in His answer. It is either Wait or No. Either one hurts me, scares me, and makes me angry.

Depression comes in, blankets me in shame, guilt and despair. How we love God when He is bringing in tangible closeness to Him, answering prayers the way we desire. How grateful we are for His presence, His mercy, His arms wrapped around us. How confused I feel, when the door to God seems to be closed.

Perhaps He is busy, perhaps He is waiting, or worse, perhaps He is angry with me. Is it not the baby in me, the one who desires to be picked up and fed immediately when she cries, confused and angered when she is not? The baby has much to learn about relationship with the parent.

I, as the baby, know not what is best for me. Not yet. Even after all my years with God, struggling and suffering, I have believed that I would be healed. Sometimes, with that as the foundation of our faith, reality is ignored. That was so until we went knocking on a human doctor's door for answers. The words were again without much hope. It was then that I chose the destiny of my days. None of us knows how long we have on this earth. So why am I allowing fear to torment me? I'm truly no sicker than I was twenty years ago when they sent me home to die. I did not die. I went on to have a life filled with all the things life brings: joy and hope, beauty and triumph, pain, loneliness and fear. The doctor we visited is only a man. God, my God, holds my life in the palm of His hand, and I have learned that it is best to live each day as if it were your last. In living that way, we leave no harsh word spoken without "I'm sorry". We speak to others as if we will never see their precious faces again. We reach out and get involved when it would be easier not to. So I'm learning in a very real way that no matter what the road, if I live my life for God, if I turn my eyes towards God and His purpose, that He will be with my tired heart until the end. Whenever that will be. In Proverbs it says that the spirit sustains the body. I am living proof of that truth.

In the midst of winter, I finally learned that there was in me an invincible summer.

Albert Camus

FOURTEEN

Winter came in as the old timers had never seen it. The land was buried under four feet of snow. The wind blew drifts to twice that. The roads closed. The water froze. The animals on the land bury themselves, and those too frail to overcome die. I bought Joey our first horse, a gray Arabian mare. He named her Lakota, and we cannot reach her. She stays up on the mountain with another horse and some cows. Joey and I begin the harsh reality of living in a fifth wheel and trying to build our home during the raging winter. We try to stay friends through the long weeks of confinement. Some days I am too sick to get up. Some days we sit in the darkened trailer, waiting for the blizzard to pass. We begin to understand the term, cabin fever. Life together is hard, as hard as the lack of water, the freezing temperatures, hauling out the trash and laundry, hauling in the groceries. After a month of phone lines going down, road closures, cars getting stuck, days without water, food shortages, fighting fevers, sore throats, body aches and shortness of breath, we move into a motel twenty miles away. At least there we have hot water, and after almost a year without, TELEVISION!

The first few days are bliss: just taking long hot baths, washing my hair, laying in bed vegetating, watching Touched By An Angel or Hallmark Hall of Fame... simple pleasures, like uniform heat, not cold pockets everywhere except right up against the space heater, cushy towels. I didn't leave that room for two days; I was exhausted. Joey would come in at the end of each day and eat stew or chili or whatever I had thrown into the crock pot that morning, then fall exhausted into bed. I became introspective and withdrawn, and felt myself to be as rigid as glass china. In truth I was feeling my frailty, and it frightened me. So I was cranky and touchy.

One week there was another blizzard, and the workers on the house shut down early to go home. Joey and I decided to head to town for supplies, to let our hair down and have a little fun. We bought a king sized bed, and groceries, and tried to see a movie, but we found we were both too exhausted. So we headed fifty-seven miles back to the motel. The snow was beginning to fall again, and it was cloudy and windy.

Joey is driving the Jeep and his driving is frightening me. Ever since we married, driving has been an issue between us. Joey has had two tickets in a year, and I have never felt that he is a defensive driver. He tends to play offense on the road; if it's his light, he takes it. I've never felt safe riding with him and we have fought about it. So I am reading a magazine instead of watching the road, trying to keep from telling him to slow down, there is black ice on the highway and I feel like he is going too fast. I put on my seat belt and try to concentrate on the magazine.

We are going down one hill and up another; I have a strange feeling in my stomach and finally I have to say something. "Joey, you're going too fast."

"I'm only going sixty miles per hour," he says, obviously irritated.

"Yeah, but it's too fast."

We are going down a hill and suddenly the Jeep begins to go out of control.

"Hold on," he says, "Come on, you son of a bitch…" He is gritting his teeth and desperately trying to gain control. We go into a three sixty spin, and as I hear Joey cursing the Jeep, I begin out loud to *praise God, praise God, praise God, praise God…*

I hear Joey say "Oh *no!*"

In slow motion we are turning, then the Jeep flips and rolls. *Praise God, praise God, praise God, praise God.*

Groceries are flying everywhere. A thick chain to pull vehicles is whipping around, the windshield is crashing in. I put my hands above my head to keep the ceiling from crashing in. In thirty seconds of time, all stands still. We have landed on our top. I am dangling by my seat belt from the top of the car. Joey has landed underneath me. I smell gas. I hear Joey say *you're OK you're OK*.

I'm not sure I am. I unhook my seat belt, shaking. I can hear people yelling, running to our aid. We are upside down in the snow and cannot get out except through the back. We crawl through the window and walk out.

"Are you OK?"

People are everywhere.

"I think so," I say. My chest and throat hurt, I am shaking uncontrollably.

"It's a miracle," I hear them saying. "We saw you go flying. It's a miracle!"

A nurse in another Jeep stops.

"Let me take you somewhere," she offers kindly… strangers are kind.

Joey is acting like some kind of he-man, asking some men to help him turn the Jeep back up on its wheels. He kicks in the ceiling. I climb into the nurse's Jeep and we leave. I see Joey in the blizzard acting like Superman.

I go back to the motel, while the nurse asks if perhaps I should go to the hospital.

The motel clerk keeps calling the sheriff's department. "We saw your Jeep, ma'am, you've been in a rollover. I think we should send an ambulance…"

I am in shock and have bruises on my arms and knees.

"Thank you, I'll stay here if you don't mind."

I crawl into a warm bath, praying. I pray and pray until two hours later the shock subsides.

Your time on earth is not through, there is work to do.

I begin to praise God. But where is Joey? Why isn't he back yet? I call the highway patrol to find out where he is. I am informed that he is en route with an officer, behind the tow truck. I hang up, and Joey walks in laughing. I am crying and hurting and angry. I am angry that he is laughing.

"I'm sorry, it's a reaction, I guess."

"Well it's not funny! For almost a year I've been telling you I don't feel safe when you're driving. You haven't listened to me. From now on *I* drive! *I'm* the driver!"

He looks at me. "I'm sorry, baby, I'm so sorry." He is holding me. "If anything bad had happened to you I don't know what I would do."

Now we are both crying.

"Thank you God for sparing our lives…"

The telephone rings, and it's the nurse who drove me to the motel.

"I just wanted to check on you and make sure you're alright."

"Thank you, you're so kind. I'm OK now, really."

I hear her sweet voice saying I can call her any time, and we hang up. Joey is rubbing my sore and achy body. We are suddenly aware of all the walls going down, and reach to hold each other close. Life is… so delicate, yet we, with the help of God, are so strong.

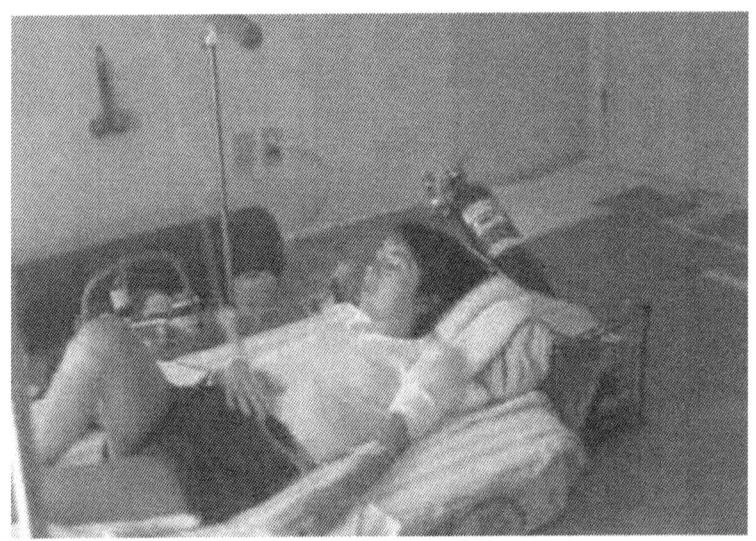

Figure 1
After pesticide poisoning 1980

Figure 2

Fishing 1958

Figure 3

Heavy Metal

Figure 4

Lynn Schriner

Figure 5
Vicky & Lynn Colorado State Fair 1998

Figure 6
View from kitchen with Lakota our Arabian

Figure 7
The House that love built

Figure 8
JJ "The kid"

Figure 9
Miss B Our "Movie Star"

Figure 10
Mom & Dad in Front of the house that love built

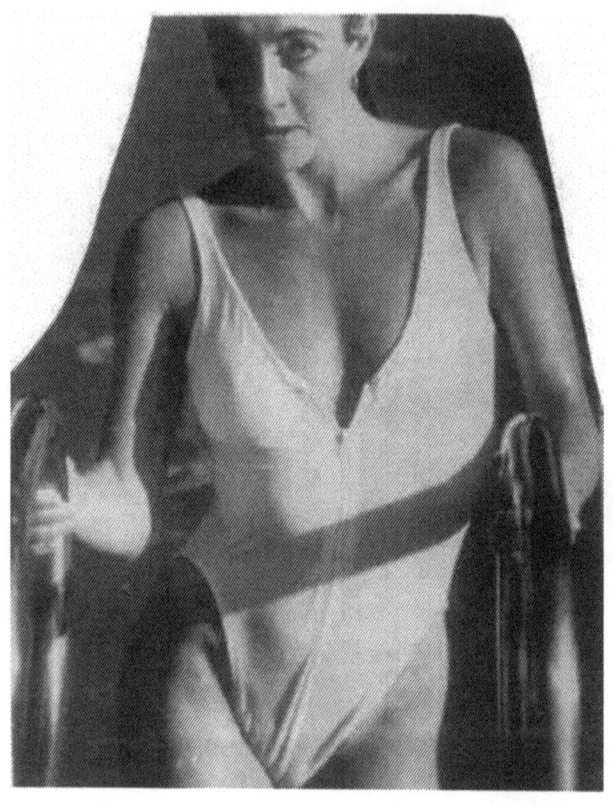

Figure 11

Figure 12
The Modeling Years
Courtesy of Randy Simon

Figure 13
Acting head shot
Courtesy of Randy Simon

Figure 14

Courtesy of Randy Simon

Figure 15

Courtesy of Randy Simon

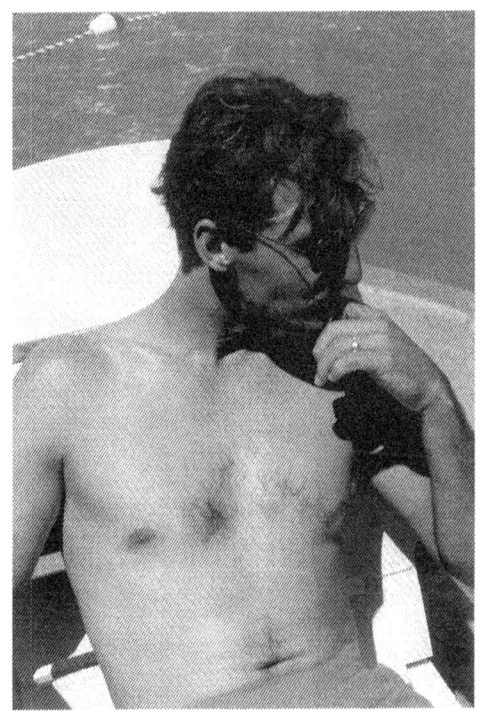

Figure 16
Joey

Figure 17
Joey

Figure 18
Lynn & Joey

Figure 19
Lynn Schriner today

It has long since come to my attention that people of accomplishment rarely sat back and let things happen to them. They went out and happened to things.

Elinor Smith

FIFTEEN

Life has held for me a thousand fleeting moments of light, where by mystery or movement or wings, my heart opens, my eyes see, my mouth tastes and my skin senses the indefinable, indescribable hand of love. It has arrived often tucked between pages of grief, novels of depression or sheets of numbness. There have been years of mostly surviving, one day after another, through pain of all colors and degrees... and then when all seems hopeless or lost there is a fleeting moment or two (or ten), of light manifesting through the faces of love.

The State Fair arrives in splendor and pageantry under a clear blue Labor Day sky. It is a small city unto itself, with food and clothing and jewelry, animals and equipment and artists and craftsmen and rides. Throughout the fair a select group of singers get to sing for half an hour at a time. Garth Brooks started at state fairs. This year I got to.

I was scheduled for one o'clock in the afternoon on the Pepsi stage. My family and friends came from all over the state and New Mexico, including my precious ninety year old grandmother, who sat in her big straw hat in a wheelchair under a large oak tree. Rarely have I seen such a beautiful sight. My mom and dad and friends sit close and fight tears as Vicky and I sing. We open with "There Goes My Heart Again" and end with "Amazing Grace," dedicated to my grandmother.

In between we sing various songs about faith and love, interacting with the crowd and with one another... All in all it was a great success.

Afterwards, kids come forward to receive a heart shaped balloon, and the sound crew come to ask if we would do another show that evening. I wanted to, but Vicky did not. So instead we mingled and ate a picnic lunch. It was after the pictures were taken and the congratulations were given that I felt my typical letdown; as if the balloon I was riding had taken a sudden drop. Friends and families scatter back to their own lives. Joey and I go back to ours: two tired people, fighting the typical problems of life. No more fantasies of fame, just reality. Two days later an ambulance drives forty miles to show up on our land. I am sitting at the hot tub, my feet immersed, shaking from fear and pain. I am strapped to a gurney and an EKG is taken. Joe and I spend the day in the hospital.   My heart grows tired and sometimes protests loudly. It is then that man and his machines intervene and I can do nothing less than turn my eyes to God, who will ride with me and my tired heart to the end.

Always do right. This will gratify some people and astonish the rest.

Samuel Clemens

SIXTEEN

One evening three years ago I walked into a Petsmart, and standing before me was the most beautiful creature I had ever seen. He was standing perfectly still, like a statue. His coat was almost blue, and his eyes, upon turning to look at me, were a jeweled green. When I walked up to him and asked his owner if I could touch him, he nudged me gently and his eyes tore into my heart. Within those eyes lay the story of the greyhound: their beauty and gentle spirit that is so abused in this country. The years of living muzzled, transported in frigid air or intense heat, in cages so small they must lie down… they cannot turn around, and there is no water. If they are lucky, they stay alone in a closed, closet sized pen.

If not, they live a hundred in a pen, muzzled, their eyes expressing their courage and magnificent hearts. After they are used up by men and women who value them only for their money making potential, they are disposed of, often shot in a field, poisoned or starved. Some are "humanely" put down at the age of four or five, healthy, beautiful, magnificent and loving. They die without ever knowing love or kindness. I didn't know any of this that first day in Petsmart, but I knew in my heart that I had to have a relationship with these animals. For my fortieth birthday, I was given Miss B, a sixty five pound blonde, gentle, easily spooked Miss B. It amazed me then and it amazes me now, the stoic courage of this animal.

All her life she had lived, isolated and unloved, in a cage or on a track. Our first year together was tough. She was, understandably, afraid of most everything, and afraid to bond with me, so we had a difficult time. She hurt herself a few times and required surgery. I was used to dogs who were *dogs*, they gave affection, and knew what the word NO meant, could be trusted to stay close.

Miss B didn't know what stairs were, or carpets or beds, had never been to a park or near a lake. When I tried to love on her, she froze like a stone.

When my precious dog Girlfriend, who had been with me for ten years, passed away, Miss B ran away from home. I was devastated by Girlfriend's death, and very hurt by Miss B's rejection. We spent a day looking everywhere for her, and for the next two days we called and went to shelters and put up posters. I felt terrible, like I had failed her, failed to love her and help her have a better life. The morning that I took her bowls and bed up off the porch and resigned myself to her loss, the phone rang. It was our neighbor Jewels, who loves animals as much as we do, someone who had been there for Girlfriend when she was put to sleep, sick with cancer. "I have a surprise for you," she said. "Miss B!" I shouted. "Miss B has come home!"

I ran down the stairs and out into the street where Jewels stood holding Miss B.

She had bloody, sore paws, and was dirty and skinny, but she had come back. I wrapped my arms around her and wept into her soft hair. She turned to me as if to say "I'm sorry" and together we climbed the stairs home. From that day forward she changed. She ate like she was hungry, slept in the bedroom at the foot of the bed. She loved to go for runs, and began to nuzzle me for loving.

Out on the land now, she is often found sunning herself on her sand pile after her daily run, her expression one of peace. We love her so much, we named our ranch after the three of us: The Jo Lyn B Ranch.

I want to adopt more greyhounds, and give them a chance to know freedom, peace and love. My prayer is that those of us who are wounded by the inhuman treatment of these splendid, sensitive and courageous animals will do everything in our power to help them. We will boycott greyhound racing, spread the word about the plight of these gentle dogs, and open our homes and hearts to them.

We are their only hope, and if given a chance, they give so much back to us.

The sun shines not on us but in us.

John Muric

SEVENTEEN

The season of winter changed and the land began to open, as if it had been withholding secrets all through the long winter. Now, with a little prodding from the sun, the bud opens and the secret of life in its center comes forth. "The house that love built" is almost complete, and Joey and I have moved in. Oh the joy of walking in socks across heated tile floors, gazing at our furniture once again, soaking in the clawfooted bathtub amidst the gleam of gold fixtures. Our new home is filled with love, from the angels that sit on shelves and peek out from crannies in the walls, to hand woven brightly yarned Mexican rugs and greenery, benches and a new king sized bed (our first marriage bed), and the windows that bring forth our mountain and the sky. By night, while Joey has slept, I have sat on the window sill as the heavenly stars, as infinite and deep as the ocean, beckon with more mysteries of God's greatness. The winter brought harsh realities of calves dying, and in this new season of life away from the city, the death of a friendship I had thought to be as strong as any love I have known. It was painful, and made me realize that relationships, no matter how intimate or endearing, will one day change. The only foundation left standing is our relationship with God.

This morning when we woke, the landscape changed once again. Instead of greenery and blue skies we had an April blizzard, complete with high winds and heavy wet snow. Joey and I missed church, and instead found ourselves driving the old pickup down a road that just yesterday had been solid and easily traveled, but now was muddy, slushy and treacherous. We pulled the truck into this groove or that pothole, trying to return rented movies and buy bread before the roads completely shut down.

Lakota can't be found out in the blizzard, so Joey and I go back to bed. Miss B and JJ, our beloved dogs, are snoozing beside the bed on the floor, chasing imaginary rabbits in their sleep as we finish reading our books, and all is well, if we can accept the circumstance of yet another storm on a spring day.

Life in the country has brought seclusion, and though we have made attempts at friendship, those in the country seem to have formed their own fences and barriers against us. We have become the object of much gossip and slander. I have never met so many two-faced people. It has hurt Joey and I, and caused a few sleepless nights, trying to figure out what we have done to cause so many to reject us.

The worst is a Vietnam vet, an alcoholic ex Green Beret mental case who lives behind us on the mountain. He rode up on a large horse one day, with a rifle across his lap, glared down at me and declared that he didn't want people moving here. I peered up at him and thought, you've got to be out of the movies, in his buckskin and hat with snakeskin and feathers. I tried to be soothing, let him know that we were the good guys, but he wasn't buying it. He has since accused us of stealing his Rotweiller (sure), and has flipped me off on more than one occasion. He has collected a bunch of rock and piled it like a grave site, putting another neighbor's name over it. He worries me, because rumor has it that he shoots when provoked.

So we try the live and let live policy, and stay to ourselves, and have days of loneliness. Our dear friends come to visit for a weekend here and there, and that keeps us going. But we pray for a couple to become close with. When I was younger I never had any trouble making friends, and most of my friends have been around for fifteen or twenty years. I always thought I was a good friend; I value friendships very highly, so rejection time and time again is new to me. It hurts, but it does draw Joey and me closer to God and to one another. We are becoming best friends through trial and stress.

My favorite quote is, "It takes pressure to make a diamond." As we become brilliant and rare...through it all, God is teaching us to shine.

He who has no fire in himself cannot warm others.

Unknown

EIGHTEEN

I used to live in an old renovated hotel in the deep pockets of Denver. It was elite, with gardens and murals and fountains, a five star French restaurant and jazz club. My apartment was wonderfully designed and featured in architectural and designer magazines. I had fully exposed thirty foot brick walls with pillared beams and ceiling fans. The hotel was occupied by artists and lawyers, doctors and salon and restaurant owners. It was an oasis in the middle of deprivation. A homeless shelter was several blocks away, winos were found passed out on the plush grass behind the building. There were drive by shootings and bars on our windows. I traded my nicer car for an old faithful Jeep Cherokee which was broken into repeatedly. I found, after living there for several months, that I had grown hardened to the pain and deprivation that surrounded the oasis. I would walk out in the morning and step over some homeless guy passed out beside my Jeep. I felt weird about doing it, but I was disconnected about it as well. Besides, I was busy doing a music video for Nashville, and had several of my works in galleries and was preparing for another show. I was having parties and dinners and riding my bike. The downtown area was a ghost town on Sundays and I loved it! It felt like it was mine.

Anyway, one day I stepped over another person on the lawn and got into my Jeep to drive away, when I heard in my head the story of Lazarus and the rich man: how Lazarus had lived outside the rich man's home and the rich man ignored him. Both died; Lazarus went to heaven, and the rich man to hell. "But Lord, I can't save them all!"

"No," I heard Him say, "But you can help one. Just pick one and reach out to him." So I did. I looked around with new eyes, and saw a man who I had noticed before because he was always alone. He lived, as best as I could tell, in the alley behind the hotel. He had an old couch that appeared to be his home, and he was often seen working on his feet. He would sit across the street with his socks off, picking and digging at his feet. It was obvious that they hurt him a great deal.

Well the first thing I did was take out a turkey dinner on a paper plate with vegetables and a roll and a big piece of cake. I approached him as he sat on his couch, he watched me as I walked towards him. "Here we are eating and I ...thought you might like some."

He reached for the plate without a word, his eyes never leaving my face.

"OK, well... Jesus loves you." I turned and left, trying to walk as if unafraid, but in truth my heart was beating quite rapidly in my chest. It started something though: I often took him food after that. A few weeks later, I went shopping and bought him a back pack, filled it with socks and medicine for sore feet, slippers and gloves, soap and toothbrush, a brush and mirror, and candy...I waited until I saw him. I walked across the street and down towards him, holding the backpack, and he watched me, yet again without a smile. I reached him where he sat on the ground.

"I brought you something," I said, and handed him the pack. He looked at me, curious.

"Well, Jesus loves you," I said, and turned to walk away. I had gone about ten steps when I heard a voice behind me say, "Hey lady."

I turned back to see him standing. "My name," he said, "Is Fred." I smiled at him.

"I'm Lynn," I said. "Nice to meet you, Fred." He lifted his hand to me and turned to walk away. I watched him walk taller, with his backpack on his back, and I thought, his name is Fred! He is somebody's kid! He had a mother who bore him, with all the hopes and dreams any mother has for their child…and I began to cry, for Fred and all the other grown up kids on the street, somebody's precious child gone terribly wrong. I felt, for a moment, God's pain for these people, who live lives of complete horror, and I vowed to help in any way I could.

Fred, meanwhile, began watching out for me. When I would walk from the Jeep into the Oasis he would rise up and with his eyes escort me safely home. Once I heard a commotion outside and looked out the window in time to see Fred move a man away from my Jeep.

My health began to deteriorate, living in a hotel over a restaurant that had to spray pesticides once a month in the kitchen. The day I moved away I looked for Fred. He wasn't in his usual place.

My prayer and hope is that we in America will adopt, through homeless shelters or churches, one of the street people, to provide a monthly donation to give food, clothing, medical attention and shelter to these people. Our hearts have become too closed. It's time we find a way to reach out to someone's Fred. They are precious to God, and we may be the only chance they have of knowing that they are not forgotten.

If you wish to donate to help the homeless, like Fred, you may send your donation to:

Damascus Ministries
P.O. Box 3134
Parker, CO 80134

Faith is the daring of the soul to go farther than it can see.

Unknown

NINETEEN

There is a mesa behind the little gray cottage where I lived in Canon City, Colorado, called Skyline Drive. I had heard when I first arrived that from the top you could see the entire Arkansas Valley. So one morning, shortly after moving in, I drove up there. I entered through stone gates announcing the road, Skyline Drive, and I thought how beautiful the arched gates were. The road, I noticed, is very narrow, and allows only one car at a time go up. It is a one way road.

The sky was blue and the day clear as I began my climb with my two dogs as companions. About halfway up I realized that there were no guard rails, and the sides dropped off in sheer cliffs on both sides of the car. I felt my palms begin to sweat and my heartbeat quickened. The car was inching forward at this point, and I kept feeling that the dogs and I were going to pitch off one side or the other and plunge to our deaths below. There were steep, sheared sides, and cracks and bumps in the road...and three quarters of the way up I couldn't see where the road was.

I began to panic, my breath grew shallow and my stomach was alive with fluttering butterflies. "Lord," I prayed, "Help me!"

My first instinct was to go back, but there was no way to turn around and, as I have stated, this was a one way road. "Lord, please!" I prayed, frightened. "Help!"

All of a sudden, the Lord began to communicate to me the valuable lesson of Skyline Drive.

This road is like life, Lynn. This road is like your faith. It is narrow and steep, and once you begin the journey you cannot go back. It is treacherous and dangerous, and often you cannot see what is in front of you. If you look to the left or the right, you could fall...but if you keep your eyes fixed on Me, if you trust Me and not your feelings, you will make it.

"Oh Lord, thank you!" I took a deep breath, calmed my shaking legs, and keeping my eyes fixed straight ahead, we made it to the top. At the top there were rocks of protection on every side, and even a place to pull over and enjoy the view. But I didn't stop, not that first time. I drove on, trusting God to lead me safely down the mountain, which of course He did. After that I drove that road five more times and stopped to see the beautiful view of the valley. I prayed for all the people in the valley, and one night I went up again to view the stars!

I overcame my fear of that road, as I have many times overcome the perils and trials of my own narrow journey on this earth, using God's message of Skyline Drive to guide me.

To not look to the left or the right...to not go back, but to keep my eyes and ears fixed on Jesus, the Author and Finisher of my faith.

*We must grow in love and to do this we must go on loving and
giving and giving until it hurts—the way Jesus did.*

Mother Theresa

TWENTY

It has been a summer of miracles. The renewing of two
vows, one with my Savior and one with Joey. Each had, through
the course of this long and painful year, endured my inconsistent
love. God remained strong, Joey had grown cold. We had lost
our friendship, lost our laughter. I no longer felt precious to him
and he felt rejected by me. We lived as strangers beneath our
longing to reach out, to overcome a year of rejection, sickness,
financial worry, constant stress and death.

We were verbally assaulted by the Vietnam vet neighbor
who had a gun, and thrown into related struggles with the legal
system to protect ourselves. We were separated by words and
circumstances, illness and stress. I had reached bottom, had
contemplated everything from suicide to divorce, and was kept
from acting on those feelings only by a tiny cord of faith. I knew
I was clinically depressed, but had been unable to take Prozac
due to toxic side effects. We lived on this beautiful land in our
new home as two people broken. God, in His infinite wisdom, let
us both reach our brokeness. We were beaten and battle
fatigued, helpless and hopeless. We had nothing left to give to
one another and our world was black.

It was then that God stepped in. I began to attend Ala-non
meetings. I called a doctor who specialized in enzyme therapy. I
began to take a precursor to tryptophane and seratonin 5HTP,
and as the levels of seratonin rose in my toxic, depleted brain, so
did my desire for life, and especially for the Giver of life. Joey
and I finally repented of all we had said and done to each other.
The feelings were real, and a marriage once dead was resurrected

under those stars. In tears and through prayer, our marriage was healed.

We began to read the Bible and pray together every day. We began to treat one another as dear and treasured friends. We began to be a "we" instead of "me". And God?

Dear God, precious, wonderful, loving God, put a hunger and a thirst for Him in our hearts. As we moved towards Him, He came closer once again. I love to talk with Him throughout the day. I love the joy I feel in His presence. Once again there is a power and an anointing when we pray for others: burdens lifted, broken bodies restored, souls come together. Life has meaning and purpose once again.

My health is still an uphill battle, but my depression has gone from a roaring lion to a small meowing kitten. I am making positive changes in my diet, my spirituality and my outlook on life. Everything is connected and everything impacts something else.

The land is changing as well. The summer's heat is slowly giving way to the season's change. The horses are beginning to grow shaggy and the acorns in the garden have fallen off the trees to the ground. All summer there has been no wind, but now it is making regular visits, tossing the horses manes and shaking the trees. I love this time of year. The sky seems to blaze blue and the sunsets are crimson. It is a time of preparation for winter: ordering the hay, stocking our cupboards, caulking the doors and windows, beginning to have need of an extra comforter on the bed at night.

Joey and I are back to dancing in the kitchen while we cook, snuggling on the couch, enjoying one another's company. We heard a wonderful analogy about love: that we make withdrawals and deposits to our love, just like a bank account.

If you make too many withdrawals and not enough deposits, you become overdrawn, and, like a bank, there are penalties to be paid. Joey and I now make a sound if one person has done or said something to hurt the other (love withdrawal): "Ching ching

ching ching," we yell out, and the other person starts to laugh. It's very comical, but it definitely gets the point across. The one responsible can then rectify the situation. It has worked great for us.

Mornings are still my favorite time of the day. The sun rises and washes our bath and bedroom with a golden glow against the palomino walls. I feel the strongest in the morning and so it is filled with activity: cleaning, laundry and dishes, hot tub, stretching and listening to music. It is my time of praise and worship, my time of hope and life. I am learning in the solitude of our times on the land, that I am strong in the Lord and the power of His might. I'm learning that with God all things are possible, if I can just override my feelings with prayer and faith. I am learning to be still in the shelter of His wings, to dance in the shadow of His presence, to stay in the light of His love.

I am the sigh of the sea, the laughter of the field, the tears of heaven.

Kahlil Gibran

TWENTY ONE

There are a few cases in my life, where what the enemy meant for evil, God has used for good. My first marriage took place in a beautiful mansion in the foothills of Colorado, on a miraculous fall day. It was a marriage out of the will of God, and it ended badly one year after we said "We do." From the ashes of pain, infidelity and adultery, a soul came to heaven twelve years later, when I visited his grandmother, who had, after a series of strokes, gone to live in a nursing home.

The day we visited, she rallied out of her stupor, became clear headed, called me by name, and accepted Christ as her Lord and Savior. She repeated the sinner's prayer with tears pouring down her weathered cheeks. I hugged her and told her I loved her, and she said in her garbled language that she loved me too.

The second time, I was in a serious relationship with a wonderful boy/man when I was eighteen and nineteen years old. We talked of marriage, lived in sin, and conceived a child that we were not ready for. Consequently the pain of that decision broke us up. He came from a large Catholic family. One of his sisters became a Christian and judged me mercilessly for the abortion.

His father, Joe, got very ill later in life, and I received phone calls from the youngest girl in the family, who had always loved me and stayed in touch. I went on and off for years to sit with the father and read the Bible to him and pray with him. In my spirit, I could feel his resistance to Jesus and God. Because of his Catholic beliefs, he never felt that he was worthy.

Many years went by and after Joey and I married, I received a phone call from the younger daughter asking if I would go and see her father in intensive care; that he was dying. I left a note for Joey, who was at work, and drove through the city streets to the hospital. I prayed all the way up the elevator and into the intensive care unit. When I entered the curtained room where he lay, I was shocked to see his swollen, bloated and bruised body. He opened one eye and saw me standing by the bed. His wife left the room to give us time alone.

"I knew you'd come," he said, his eyes misting.

"Of course, Joe. I had to see you and say good bye."

He looked at me and terror filled his eyes.

"Are you afraid to die, Joe?" I asked him, holding his hot and swollen hand.

"Yes." He began to cry.

"What about all the times we talked and prayed about Jesus, do you still not believe?"

He was crying, "I'm not worthy. I've done bad things."

Just then my husband came in and stood beside me. After introducing the two, we held Joe's hands and began to talk about the sacrifice and the atonement of Christ's blood for our sins. *All* have sinned and fallen short of the glory of God, and it is only through Christ's blood that any of us get to heaven to be with God.

"All you have to do is confess your sins and ask Jesus to be the Lord of your life, Joe; are you ready to do that now?"

He looked into my eyes, which were filled with the love of God. I could *feel* God's mercy and love coming right through me to this lost and dying man. Joe took my hand and squeezed it tight, and my husband took my other hand and squeezed it tight, and I led Joe in the confession of sin and the acceptance of the risen Lord.

He visibly relaxed. "I'm not afraid any more," he said.

The next day he died. At the funeral, the Christian daughter came to me with tears in her eyes and thanked me for what I had been able to do with her father. I believe he is now singing with the angels, along with my aborted baby, his grandchild, in heaven.

*There are only two ways to live your life: one, as if everything
is a miracle, and the other, as if nothing is.*

Albert Einstein

TWENTY TWO

It was winter 1982, and I was living in Arizona with my brother, to give my parents a much needed break from caring for me. I weighed about eighty five pounds and was quite ill. The desert, with its climate change, had changed my brother's health dramatically for the better. He had wanted me to come and try it out and so I had. Despite everyone's best intentions I had grown much worse, and my days were endless.

One Saturday morning I went to the kitchen to get water while my brother was out in the garage working on his BMW. The five gallon glass container sat on the kitchen counter. Tipping it to fill my jug, it slipped from my hands and came crashing down. First it hit my ankle, which promptly broke, and as it shattered to the tile floor, a large piece of glass flew up and cut my artery wide open. I looked down at my foot and the blood which was gushing from the open wound, and said one word, "Jesus." A peace descended over me as I grabbed a dish towel and shoved it into the wound. Between the water and the blood, the kitchen looked like a massacre had occurred. I crawled out to the front steps, and in a very weak voice began to call out to my brother for help. He was waxing the car with a power tool and could not hear me. Growing weaker by the minute, I continued to call out, "Help me. Help...help." Suddenly a neighbor came stumbling out onto her front porch in her curlers and bathrobe, searching for the newspaper. She turned to me.

"Oh my GOD! What do you want me to do?"

"Please go get my brother," I said peacefully. I watched her run, bathrobe flying.

Then my brother came running back, his eyes filled with horror as he saw me surrounded with blood.

"Shit! Shit! What do you want me to do?" he asked, clearly frightened. Why was everyone asking me?

"I need to go to the hospital," I said.

He grabbed me, picked me up and ran for his beloved BMW. Putting me inside, he took off, running lights, going down the middle of the avenue. I turned to look at his dear face.

"You'd better slow down or we might die before we get there."

We pulled into emergency and I was rushed inside. The doctors and nurses all rushed around me examining and questioning.

"We have to operate," the doctor said. "Your artery needs to be closed and the ankle set."

"OK, but I can't have anesthesia or painkillers or antibiotics, because I am allergic to them."

Everyone stopped and stared at me in horror and then at my brother, who was nodding in confirmation. "Call my doctor in Denver," I said. "He'll explain it to you."

The doctor left with the number in his hand, and I went immediately to prayer.

"Lord, it's me again. Things aren't looking very good, but I know that I can get through anything with you. If you want me to go through the surgery I will, but if you can heal me another way, please make it perfectly clear. Amen."

At that point the doctor came back, looking pale. "We have no choice," he said.

"We have to operate."

"OK," I said. "Let's go."

I said goodbye to my brother and we headed into the operating room. There they began to prep me for surgery. As the surgeon began to reach into my open wound searching for glass, I cried out and then moaned. "Got a bullet to bite on?" I asked.

There was no answer. Tentatively the surgeon went in again. I thought, "I don't think I can handle this after all." Suddenly the surgeon threw his instrument down. "I can't do this!" he said.

"Praise GOD!" I said, "You won't have to." This was my sign! God had another way!

The hospital cleaned the wound, sutured it and braced it, and I requested to go home, because a hospital is the worst place for an immune suppressed person to be, with all the germs and cleaning chemicals. They looked at me as if I had lost my mind.

After signing a release, my brother loaded me back into the car and drove me home. That night, and for weeks after, the pain was of a caliber I cannot describe. Without painkillers of any kind, an I.V. in my arm for nourishment, and a daily visit from a neighboring doctor my parents had hired to come and change the dressings, I went through days of total torture. My brother had to return to school and work, so I was left alone for eight to ten hours a day. The days were long, and the Bible and the 700 club with Pat Robertson were my only company. The lowest point of my life came when I, unable to make it to the bathroom or bedpan, lost control of my bowels and had to lay in it on the bed all day until my brother came home to clean me up. "Lord!" I cried out. "Take me now! I can't live like this! It can't get any worse. I hate my life!"

If I thought it couldn't get any worse, I was mistaken. Three weeks after the accident, I developed a terrible infection. The doctor from next door came over and promptly told me that I had to be in a hospital. "I can't," I said, "You don't understand." She said, "Without treatment, you could die."

I began to cry. "You don't understand. The antibiotics will kill me for sure!"

"I'm calling your parents," she said angrily. "I wash my hands of this." I heard her storm out of the house and slam the door. The silence was deafening, and my despair was great. Where was God? Where was His promise that He would heal me without man's intervention? "Lord, I can't bear another minute of this pain!"

My glands were swollen, and there were red streaks running up my leg. I had a high fever and was in utter despair. "Where are you, Lord? Help me!" I cried, sobbed and pleaded, "Help me, Lord!"

Suddenly the despair and the depression I had been feeling left me completely, and I was left with joy! My fever was still there, the leg was still infected, but the despair was gone. I began to praise Him. "Thank you, Lord. Oh praise You, oh thank you…"

I began to sing praises to God and continued for about an hour. Then, just as suddenly, I heard…an audible Voice in the room, ***Get up and walk.***

I stopped praising Him and peered into the morning light streaming into the bedroom where I lay. "Is that You, Lord?" But I knew it was, and I knew I had to act. My foot, which had been elevated for almost a month, was throbbing and swollen. Gingerly I took it off the elevated pillow, and the throbbing increased. I gritted my teeth to keep from passing out as the leg came down, and the blood rushed into it like slow motion. "Lord!"

But the moment my foot touched the floor, the *moment* I stood on His word and pushed up off the bed to …*walk*… all the pain, all the infection, all the fever was gone! I was totally healed. I stomped my foot, I searched it, I tore off the brace and the bandages. There were two beautiful stitched scars and NO PAIN. I was healed.

I ran around praising God and weeping for joy. My God is not a liar! He promised me healing and He delivered! I ran outside and banged on the doctor's door. She opened it and turned completely white. "Jesus healed me!" I grinned. "See?"

She turned angry. "Whatever!" she said, and slammed the door shut in my face.

Shortly afterwards she moved away. "Oh Lord, why can't people believe?" I knew the truth, and the truth had set me free!

When my brother returned that night from school, I was vacuuming and cooking for him. He turned pale. "What happened?" he asked, aghast.

"Jesus," I answered, smiling. "Dear Jesus."

Truth needs no crutches.

Unknown

TWENTY THREE

When I first came out of the years of isolation, in and out of hospital beds, first in a protected isolation ward with filtered air and water, where gowned and masked nurses and visitors attended to me. I was frightened, and so young... then, after a month without improvement, my mom and I boarded a plane for Chicago, and another week of living in a mental hospital while they ran all kinds of tests to determine my nutritional status. During my stay in the hospital, my two roommates were diagnosed with schizophrenia. One tried to kill me, tearing out her I.V. and swinging the bottle around the room, then going for me. At eighty five pounds, I was too weak to get up, so my dear mother threw herself over me as a shield until the orderlies came and put the girl in a straitjacket and took her to isolation. That night, a large boy came into my room and stood over me in the dark. I lay there not knowing what he was doing and highly uncomfortable. He left without incident, until the next day when my mother was with him in the cafeteria. He was weeping, and when my mom went to comfort him, he took a swing at her. All the while I was witnessing to my other roommate about Jesus and His love. We prayed the sinner's prayer together, and she and her mother left radiant. It was a time of peace in the midst of a very confusing storm.

Whenever we looked at our surroundings, it was a terrifying place of unreality, much like a Salvador Dali painting. But when I could come out of my circumstances and introspection, and see the deep needs of others, and allow Christ to flow from me into their hearts, it was a blanket of God's love, a triumph of God's peace. Each time I have gone through an experience, seeing another side to life, I have had the opportunity to be God's heart, to be His eyes and hands, to reach out and touch a hurting soul with His love, and I have grown. I would have, in my flesh, preferred to be Amy Grant, but I have been given a life, a life that has been used to lead others to God, to direct and point the way to the greatest love that is ever known. If I have despaired at my circumstance , I have rejoiced at the tremendous relationship that I have been privileged to know. I stay close to God in pain, and God has been faithful to see me through.

Judge not your friend until you stand in his place.

Unknown

TWENTY FOUR

I was a teenager during the late sixties and early seventies. It was a time of defying the established laws and rules that had governed people for so long. No sex out of marriage became sex with anyone and everyone. Free love. I was a Beatles fan and I protested the war in Vietnam. I was taught by my peers that having sex made you popular. School was unnecessary, just a function of the establishment to brainwash you. So I went into a free thinking hippy world of drugs and alcohol, sex and rock 'n' roll. The dress was platform shoes and bellbottoms, Nixon was lying and bombing Hanoi. I was seeing movies like A Clockwork Orange, The Exorcist, and Last Tango In Paris. I lived out of marriage in a canyon in the mountains. We ate zucchini and rice and tuna, sunbathed naked, wrote poetry and music, and dabbled in tarot and white witchcraft. I was as lost as I could be. During the course of those years I became pregnant, more than once, and with the pregnancies came abortions. The horror of a life taken from your womb leaves you scarred. Still, as a young free thinking girl, you move on, trying to forget the pain of that loss and the trauma of such a procedure.

Later, much later, after I became a Christian, I found deliverance from the scars. The pulpit often preaches that abortion is murder, and that those of us who have had abortions are murderers. Before I was delivered, I would shrink into my seat, full of shame and torment, unable to receive forgiveness or forgive myself. I would hear the words hopeless sinner, and run from the very God who could and would heal me. It was Satan's strategy to keep me from God's plan. I saw the hatred and the judgment in most Christians' eyes. I heard the anger and the murder in their own hearts for those who perform abortions, and I thought about the wrath of God. I lost sight of the love of God, until one day God said *It is time to be set free, my child, and I will use you to set others free.*

I went into prayer. I was with a trusted spiritual Christian woman, and as we began to pray the Lord began to move. I had a vision of my babies in heaven, in the arms of Jesus Christ my Lord. I began to weep, desperate haunting tears.

Shame and grief poured down my face, years of locked rooms were suddenly thrown open, and I felt every hidden heartbreak. The Lord and the babies waited in peace and serenity as I poured out my shame, my guilt and my pain. "I'm so sorry, I loved you so much. I didn't know what else to do. I was a girl, no one encouraged me to have you, I was so afraid and so weak. Please forgive me," I howled. A peace settled on me. The babies somehow conveyed to me that they were happy and that they forgave me. It was a complete healing for me. To know without a doubt that they are in heaven with Jesus, and that they forgave me, set me free.

Since that time the Lord has used me to set other women free. One night I was leaving church, and a young beautiful girl was weeping by the back window. I felt so drawn to her; the Lord was all over me.

"Are you alright?" I asked her.

"No, something has happened and I don't know if I can live with it." The Lord spoke to me in my inner spirit. *She has had an abortion.* When the Lord speaks to you like that it is called revelation knowledge.

"Let's go out to my car and pray," I said boldly. When the Lord is on me I often get very bold.

She looked at me undecided. I took her arm, and wrapped my arms around her waist. We went out into the night to the parking lot and my car. "I've had an abortion," she wailed. "I don't know if the pain will ever go away." I was able to comfort her because I had been there. "Let's pray," I said, taking her hand. The Lord took us to the same vision. "Can you see Jesus?" I asked, "With your baby?"

"Yes…" she cried.

"Do you see your baby in Jesus' arms?"

"YES!"

"Is there anything you want to tell your baby boy?" Suddenly the Lord spoke to me and to the girl in my car. "Oh, I'm sorry," I said, amazed. "It's a little girl!"

"I know," she cried. "Oh, my baby girl, I am so sorry! I love you so much. Please forgive me! Lord Jesus, please forgive me!" the peace of God began to settle in the car. The vision faded, the girl was calm, and the spirit of the Lord rested on her face.

"You are free now," I said. "Praise the Lord!"

"I know," said the girl. "It's finally over." That beautiful girl has gone on to ministry school, healed by the forgiving love and truth of Jesus Christ. *You shall know the truth, and the truth will set you free.*

From your parents you learn love and laughter, and how to put one foot in front of the other.

Helen Hayes

TWENTY FIVE

I see my parents pulling up the drive, bearing food of course, both for the body and for the soul. I see sometimes the silver and the slowness, and for a moment the unsteady shaking of my mother's hands. I love her hands. They were always so long and slender, beautiful and strong, and mine were short and squatty like my father's. Everything about my mother was long and strong with grace; she was regal like a queen, and sometimes she was cold like a matriarch. It was her defense, her chill. Her body would become sharp lines and rigid, like holding a thin tree trunk. She was beautiful. Our family pictures reflect the façade of health, and none of the frailties of sickness, which is part of the marriage vows my parents met head on in the night. Children who wound up with the genetic pool of pain, not the freedom of wholeness. Our world growing up revolved around needles, and medicine, and oxygen, and doctors, and special diets and constant monitoring. I looked to my mom for reassurance and strength that only she, in her protective armor, could give. But armor keeps one at a distance, because the measure of armor is its protection from outside impact. That seemed at times to include a small girl who had need of a warm bosom and a soft lap to crawl into.

My father is the quieter one. He seems more approachable and has softer lines on his face. He shouldered the world and never cried, except when he fell down the stairs, and the other time when he watched me record a song about God in the aftermath of hell. He has let me come closer without walls so obvious, but his walls are distant in his heart. I always thought he was a great listener, but often I see his "listening" is his ability to be in two places at once. It's OK, I somehow always felt I had to protect him from my life, because he hurts more deeply and doesn't sense that I know how to share his pain. He adores my mother, and they are beautiful together. They made quite handsome children, my mother made a handsome house, and we often ate meals served like Martha Stewart prior to her years on television. My mother was born with style and my father basked in her abilities. He brought to the family the simpler things of life: a day on the river with a pole, a beer, football, and blue jeans. My mother guided and directed the home, picked out my father's clothes, and he brought in the money. We had everything we needed and often more than we wanted. If they went without to give us those things they never made mention of it, and as the years went by my mother's shrewd financial head and Dad's hard work and well earned reputation brought more money than was needed. The rest multiplied in a far off company under the watchful eye of their financial manager.

They now live well in the years of silver hair and lined faces. They travel and move about and have generously given to me and my husband as we struggle with the rip tides of health, jobs, and the ever increasing cost of living. We watch them come up the walk to our front door; they smile and kiss us, and marvel at the sunshine and the soft breeze. They come to hear of our lives which I, of late, hate to share, because our world has crashed in spite of their generous and thoughtful care. I reflect on how often I have wished that dreams for one's children would be all that was necessary to ensure a quality life. That I, their daughter, who loves them so but somehow has had to go an uphill course, could do one thing on this earth with success…that they could tuck away into their hearts, and die at peace about their children, instead of worrying that the garden they so lovingly planted over forty years ago might not ever bear any fruit.

Perhaps they don't view me that way at all. Perhaps they understand that my fruit is more in the patients who came sick and left well, in the children I have befriended, and in the prayers I have prayed for others. In the fact that I have lived through so much pain, the fact that I love them so, and have found beautiful friends, and have a sensitive heart, instead of a six figure income and two grandkids. I like to believe that they feel that way too, because above all else, they are good people, with their own hurts and fears and shattered dreams, who have always, I believe, tried their very best. I think that is all family is truly about, becoming separate entities, but bound by blood and hearts and dreams for one another, regarding one another as strong enough to make it on one's own, but choosing not to, because commitment to the end is the true mark of love. I love knowing that after my parents leave today, they will take home a piece of our love and we will keep a piece of theirs. That our home can be their home if they choose, and their smiles, their love and support will always feel like home to me.

The poor are God's gift; they are our love.

Mother Teresa

TWENTY SIX

I sat in the morning light and watched the birds fly to the feeder in the tall trees of our small grove we called the forest. The pine smell hung thick in the air. It was what my world had narrowed to, lingering within the hands of death, yet still alive, still prayerful, and some days even hopeful that there was more for me here on earth. More than this irregular heartbeat and swimming headaches. More than the constant treatments to keep my body stabilized, more than laying lethargic and aching in the morning light watching tree branches sway in the wind. If only God would take me out of my introspection of pain, if only I could rise out of the last year's battle of disease and find purpose. I felt in my cry to God, a lift, for a brief moment, as if angels' wings had flown from my extended and withered hand, straight to heaven, and the prayer had taken flight and was answered.

The answer came that very morning, as my father came to help me, and brought with him a newspaper article. They called her "Aspen's angel for Haiti" and after my father encouraged me to read the story of this beautiful woman and her orphaned babies and children, I felt completely covered in the peaceful presence of the Holy Spirit, saying gently, "Call her, offer your help, pray for her, reach out." I remember dialing the foundation's phone number and speaking with a secretary. "I know you must be overwhelmed with phone calls," I said, "but I would like to help." There was a pause at the other end of the phone.

"You're the first phone call we've had from the article," she said softly.

"You're kidding me!" I was astonished. Was no one else moved by this beautiful girl and her suffering children?

I wrote her a letter, sent her money and prayed. I prayed for the orphans, for the ministry, and for the girl. Her story had touched me in a place I knew well. She had been, the article said, in Playboy magazine, a model for sixteen years, and she had been sexually molested as a child. She had some of my past, some of my pain, and she had my heart for the suffering. I would pray for her, and send her all the money I could, as often as I could. I felt God's gentle presence whenever I prayed for her, and I felt called to serve God by praying for this tender spirit. It was enough to pull me from my own suffering for a while each day, to remember these precious, orphaned and completely poverty stricken children. Whenever I felt sorry for myself I would find myself praying for these babies, and convicted that, though I suffered, it could be so much worse. That truly I had so much!

It hit home with me every time I prayed. I prayed for this beautiful girl's protection, and for her heart to stay courageous, and for God to move on her behalf for all of the children's needs. I am now trying hard to raise awareness for the orphans in Haiti. In a small way, they have become my babies too, and I share with Susie Krabacher, a lifelong commitment to the heart of Jesus Christ for these lost and suffering children. Through her Foundation for Worldwide Mercy and Sharing, Susan and her precious husband Joseph raise enough money and donate enough of their own time and money to feed over sixteen hundred children per day. They have an orphanage for handicapped children, a school, a feeding center and several part time medical clinics.

Susie was given another orphanage and school by an elderly voodoo priest, who after observing Susie and her work for many years, said, "Send me the white woman," upon whom she bestowed nine hundred healthy orphans from the mountains outside of Port-Au-Prince.

Thus is the story of a girl who was willing to follow the calling on her heart, and the beauty of knowing a true "angel on earth" whose determination and courage have made a difference in the lives of the precious children in Haiti.

To contribute to the feeding and tender loving care of the sixteen hundred orphans, please send your check or money order to:

The Foundation for Worldwide Mercy and Sharing
201 North Mill Street Suite 201
Aspen, Colorado 81161-1557

All the money you share (every last cent of it) goes to the children! None of it is used for administrative costs. That comes out of the generous hearts of Joe and Susie Krabacher.

God gives us wings when we least expect it.

TWENTY SEVEN

I am sitting in the doctor's office twenty-seven months after the roll-over. I have been once again through hell and back. We lost our jobs down south, my office closed and my patients given other options through a letter that spoke my heart, because my own health had failed. I didn't want to close the office, but we had no choice. Joey had once again come through for me in the Lord, and moved me up north to be closer to doctors. It began with blackouts while driving, and irregular heartbeats so bad that I couldn't walk to the bathroom without assistance. We lived in hotels paid for by my parents. We lived off friends who gave selflessly with checks tucked into cards. I lived for prayer, because I felt death was imminent. I gasped for air, the room was constantly spinning, my heart was pounding and irregular, and I was humbled, brought deeper down. I beseeched God to touch me or let me die. I had not the strength to endure.

My parents bought us a travel trailer. We go from state park to state park, from doctor to doctor. We live from breath to breath, prayer to holy prayer, life narrowed. I suffer from apnea at night, struggling to come to consciousness and take a breath, my body shuddering, my brain fogged and unable to grasp. I crawl outside and cry out to God. For months I have no sleep of normalcy. I sit up night after night and cry out and pray and read the Bible and seek God's face.

Each night feels like my last. My parents have come home to care for me so that Joey can go back to work.

We spend our days in treatments at doctors' offices, fighting despair, trusting God. Through it all He keeps calling me to holiness. If I am sharp with my tongue He convicts me to sorrow and sorry's (repentance).

The doctors have diagnosed me with a brain stem injury, a bruised and injured heart, and a twisting of my cartoid artery. In addition, I am fighting off the effects of herbicides and pesticides applicated everywhere, T.B. in my bones and Epstein Barr virus in my system. It is truly only God who can put me back together. If we believed in traditional, conventional medicine, I would be in intensive care, but I do not wish to live my life that way. So I go daily to a chiropractor who specializes in kinesiology, N.E.T. and N.A.E.T. treatments. I see two of these men, one a Christian, both caring and compassionate. They work with me and are on call to me. One of them has come to us several times when I was in crisis, to stabilize me. I will never forget his kindness.

Slowly, I begin to stabilize, feel stronger, and have less heart episodes. Through God's leading, we find that my body, through all the trauma, has done an auto immune response. I have literally become allergic to my own organs, blood, tissue and chemicals. After each treatment some symptoms leave the menu. I no longer have aching bones or sleep apnea. I have more energy, but still my mind is injured. I have not been able to drive for over a year. I have gone to a neuro-optometrist who specializes in brain/eye injuries. I have memory problems, feel clouded, and when traveling in a moving auto, my eye cannot track all of the movement coming at me. It is at this point that I feel my eyes roll and I get dizzy; the world swims. If I can't close my eyes then, I will pass out. It is in this shape that I have been scanned, poked and viewed by several doctors specializing in brain injuries. Their findings are: significant injury to the brain stem, resulting in optical/memory and functional problems.

They recommend six to eight months of rehab wearing specialized glasses and retraining the eye/brain connection. The prognosis is poor.

It is in this place that God moves in and heals the brain stem. I awaken one morning and hear God speak for me to do some neuro tests on myself that had been performed in the doctor's office, such as walking heel to toe, and standing on one foot and closing my eyes. In the past I had fallen during those tests. Today I stood in the morning light and walked heel to toe perfectly. I then tried standing on one foot and closing my eyes. I stayed stable, solid as a rock.

I was excited, and for days I praised God and made quiet statements of faith. I knew something had been healed, I felt different. I knew God had touched me, but I wanted to let it take its course without any man's input.

I've come today for my first appointment in rehab after we got the OK from the insurance company that they would cover everything. I'm sitting next to a young woman and her son, who are undergoing treatments, and another woman is seated across from me. The nurse steps forward and says the doctor is ready to see me. I go in, and after we exchange pleasantries, I ask if he will do another exam, because something has been healed between now and two months prior.

He asks what I have been doing, have I gotten the special prescription filled? I say no, that I have done nothing but pray. He looks at me strangely and says, "Well let's see."

He runs his tests, and all, *come back normal.* At this point he is dumbfounded. I can see that he is disturbed and perplexed. "They don't teach this in medical school," he growls. "In thirty years I have never seen anything like this." He then calls his assistant in while I am praising God out loud in his office.

"We'd better figure out what she has, because if everybody had this we'd be out of business." He is looking at his assistant as I am grinning like the Cheshire Cat and praising Jesus Christ.

"But be sure to fear the Lord and serve Him faithfully with all your heart.
Consider what great things He has done for you."
1 Samuel 12:24

"What does she have?" his assistant asks. I look at her. "Jesus Christ."

She winks at me and turns back to the doctor. "I have that," she says.

"Well, what's wrong with you; why can't you do this?" he asks. He then turns to me. " Why did this God make you suffer for so long?"

I take a breath, and wait for God to speak through me to this angry, confused man. "This is the God who does things like hang His own Son on the Cross, crucified, for three days before He is resurrected, to save you and me. I don't see that God does things in ways that we would perceive as "easy." Jesus took all my sins and yours on His own body as He hung there. The whole world turned black, without light as He gave up His life." I am moved to my feet. The doctor is not ready to receive this awesome truth. He looks at me. "Well, see you. You don't need us."

I look back at him. "Please don't forget me and what you have seen."

He is aghast and snorts, " That's not likely."

I left with Joey, after testifying to the two women sitting in the waiting room. The very next day, I began driving. As the symptoms of dizziness came, I claimed God's promises. "I can do all things through Christ who strengthens me." And I drove on. The dizziness cleared.

Why did God wait, until years of seeking help led me to the door of a doctor who stated two months prior that the prognosis was poor and man had declared support both financially and medically? It is not entirely for us to know.

Regardless, God has still left me symptoms and other roads to travel, just like that night in the trailer years before when he healed my foot, but left more serious problems seemingly untouched, and years' more suffering ahead. With the humbled knowledge of His touch, His hand on my life, and His heart fixed on me as mine has been on Him, I face each day trusting Him to carry out His purpose in my life.

There are days when I am awash with peace and confidence that all is well with my soul, and days when I must fight fear when the pain grows deep and strong.

I wait, I pray, I trust and I struggle, but ultimately I know, He is everything and in Him is everything I need. So I learned to seek the Giver of Gifts and not just the Gifts themselves. The answer to every need is Jesus. As I've learned to let go and not wonder if my life has a meaning, or whether I am seeing the backside of my journey. I am learning to shift my point of view to see that I don't have to know exactly how to dance through my life, but that I can put my feet on God's feet, my hands in Jesus' hands, and slowly, He is teaching me to dance.

Lynn Schriner

We have no right to ask when a sorrow comes, "why did this happen to me?" unless we ask the same question for every joy that comes our way.

Phillip Bernstein

EPILOGUE

When we returned to the city, it was now two million people. We moved twenty six miles out, on two and a half acres in the pines, and found peace. The neighbors on this street where we live are pleasant and friendly; we have a yearly Christmas party and they come smiling. The house that love built sits empty now, the lessons taught through this process were painful and powerful, etched forever on my heart, which is remarkably healed.

My days are quiet. I awaken to the early morning light to send Joey off to work, to feed the animals, to spend time with God... to keep hearing the Voice that gently calls my name. I find the sunsets here are equally beautiful, and the birds I feed sing sweetly (though I do miss the meadowlark). Each day I awaken with the newness of hope. The treatments that I am undergoing are working God's work, and I am being healed. There has been reconciliation with Joe's family, and thoughts and desires for a family of our own.

Life is a constant unfolding adventure. It still causes me to tremble at its touch. I am still moved by its suffering. I am still tempered by its love, and I can only continue to wait, as the Maker and Lover of my soul leads me ever on. As I go through my days, still expectant, still grateful I know, that through it all, in His perfect will "I was born for a time like this."

Lynn Schriner

Appendix

To order *Bent, Not Broken* :

Contact 1stbooks Library at 1.888.280.7715,
Or email them at 1stbooks@1stbooks.com .
Their website may be found at www.1stbooks.com .
Access to the 1stbooks Library is available through Barnes &
Noble Bookstores.

Lynn Schriner is available for speaking and singing
engagements. For booking information email Lynn at
weaselway@netzero.net . Or write to her at:
P.O. Box 3134
Parker, Colorado 80134.

To contact Lynn's doctors for N.A.E.T. Bioset treatment
information:

Dr. Jeffrey Landis
10439 Quivas
Northglenn, CO 80234
303.457.9544

For N.E.T. , kinesiology and Chinese medicine:

Dr. Craig Stimpson
6000 East Evans Bldg 3 Ste. 010
Denver, CO 80222
303.691.1771

To support the homeless in America (like Fred), send your tax deductible check or money order to:

Damascus Ministries
P.O. Box 3134
Parker, CO 80134

To help support the orphans in Haiti, send your tax deductible check or money order to:

Worldwide Mercy and Sharing
201 North Mill Street Suite 201
Aspen, CO 81611-1557

For more information on the greyhounds and how to help them, contact:
Greyhound Pets of America   1.800.366.1472

To become involved in the grassroots effort to protect us all (water, animals and kids) from pesticides, contact:

Mothers & Others (Meryl Streep's organization)
40 West 20th Street
NY, NY 10011-4211
Mothers@mothers.org

Rachel's Environment
www.rachel.org

Greenpeace
www.greenpeace.org

Lynn Schriner

God bless you as you follow your heart.

Never doubt that a small group of committed people can change the world, for in fact that is all that ever has.

Eleanor Roosevelt

About the Author

Born and raised in the west, Lynn Schriner has had an extraordinary life. She has gone from a rock singer in Europe to a naturopathic doctor. From a model to an artist, to a talk show host. From a wild child to a christian. Her motto is "it takes pressure to make a diamond." She is currently living outside of Parker, Colorado, with her husband Joe and their critters.